The Technique of
Portrait Painting

Plate 1. *In this head, the areas of flesh in shaaow were painted with umber, ultramarine blue, and a little yellow ochre. White, ochre, and a little umber were used for the light passages. This is an example of the subtle, yet rich color range that can be achieved with a limited palette that excludes red.*

The Technique of Portrait Painting

by Frederic Taubes

Watson-Guptill Publications   New York

Other Books by Frederic Taubes

Contents

Introduction

You might wonder how the present book differs from my earlier presentations on the subject. The answer is rather obvious: the experience of almost four decades of teaching has brought about a definite clarification of the issues involved in the discipline of portrait painting. When I mention *discipline*, I can as well refer to *science*, for there can be little doubt that the methodology of my teaching has been developed along scientific (that is, pragmatic) lines. So I have endeavored to develop these methods as completely as possible for the benefit of the serious art student.

Conventions of portrait painting

Those who are acquainted with my technical writings will—justly—at once equate "perfection" and "completeness" with the techniques used by the great masters of the past.

When we inquire whether the modern school has had anything to contribute to the ancient discipline of portrait painting, the answer is —absolutely nothing. There has been no technical innovation in portraiture during the past 500 years. In terms of technique, the art of painting has been in decline since classical methods were generally cast aside during the latter part of the 19th century. As to the esthetics of portraiture, the modern school has made a radical break with conventions by disavowing tradition. But portraiture *can* rest on

premises that have their roots in convention alone.

Consider the human countenance, for example: as soon as it combines (as it obviously must) two eyes, as many ears, but only one nose, one mouth, etc., it is a conventional affair. And as soon as you are out to render these conventions faithfully (more or less), you must recognize that you are treading an inherently conventional path.

Learning from the great masters

When I refer to *classical* methods (leaving all semantic interpretations aside) , we can say that implicit in the term *classic* are the highest standards of achievement from the past. Now, the past which concerns us stretches over five centuries, during which several classical periods superseded one another. Which of these periods should guide us in our search for the best possible synthesis of conception and technique?

It goes without saying that the detailed conception and amazingly precise technique of a Van Eyck (early 15th century) would not be feasible in our time because of stylistic (not technical) reasons. And the same could be said of the conceptions current during the Italian Renaissance, although some features inherent in that style could be incorporated into contemporary work.

Proceeding chronologically, we may consider

the art of Rubens (17th century), Gainsborough (late 18th century), and Goya (late 18th and early 19th century) as paradigms of great classic portraiture from which the contemporary painter *may* derive much knowledge and inspiration. One other name—a portraitist of highest rank—should be mentioned: Degas (late 19th and early 20th century).

And now you may ask, what about Rembrandt, the portraitist par excellence? Of course I am well aware of him, and of all the other great names not mentioned here; as a matter of fact, a step by step account of all the methods used by the great masters was minutely described in my book, *The Mastery of Oil Painting*. But, in this treatise, I am concerned with examples which could be of practical value to the *contemporary* portraitist.

I mentioned Degas as the last on our list of "teachers"; wherein lies the value of his teaching? He demonstrates the essential virtue of discretion, if you will, in his treatment of his subjects. Here we have arrived at the crux of the matter: *discretion*. By this term I mean the avoidance of the obvious and trivial that mars so much contemporary portraiture.

My experience in portraiture

At this point, the reader who is not conversant with my work may want to know something about my own professional history in the field of portraiture.

After leaving the Bauhaus in Weimar, where I graduated as an abstract painter shortly after the end of World War I, I discovered that although a lot of people talked about abstractions, very few wished to put them on their walls. Luckily, I remembered my thorough training in draftsmanship, which started early in my childhood, and my capacity, acquired later as a teenager, to paint people "as they appear in life." Consequently, I started to paint portraits as an assured means of making a living, and for some eight years (in the twenties) I traveled on and off all over Eastern Europe, painting literally hundreds of commissioned portraits, besides being active on

the Viennese exhibition scene as a painter of semi-abstract subjects.

In 1930, at the outset of the Great Depression, I found myself in the United States, in the role of a society portraitist. (There never seems to be a depression in the line of portraiture.) After ten more years as a successful portraitist, a profession I practiced as a sideline to my "general" painting activity, I gave up portraiture. My reason was simple: being a society portraitist is a time-consuming business —too much time is spent on sociability rather than on the pursuit of art—and I found the latter more rewarding.

Ingredients of successful portraiture

What will lead you to successful portraiture? First and foremost, *proper draftsmanship*; for without that, success in the conventional art of portrait painting is impossible. Surely the expressive conception of human and animal forms or a landscape need not rely on the painter's capacity to render a *likeness*. Simulating natural appearances can have artistic merit even when done by unschooled hands. But, in traditional portraiture, a satisfactory likeness has to rely on the artist's capacity to reproduce his models with a sufficient degree of faithfulness.

Hence, before entering into the discussion of the ways and means of portrait painting, I shall instruct you first in the basic structure of the human face and body. This will give you a pattern, a conceptual certainty, so to speak, about the object of your investigation.

One more observation. Experience teaches us that some people are born with a capacity— a knack—for achieving a likeness. There are "born" portrait painters. However, this does not necessarily assure their artistic performance. Other people acquire this capacity through assiduous application, perseverance, and proper training.

My own long training as an analyst of paintings in their historic context reveals a curious finding: the more imagination a painter possesses, the more difficult it is for him to objectively gather "facts" as they present themselves to his eye. Conversely, a *lack of imagination* allows the painter to concentrate on the image with greater accuracy. These conditions we find manifestly present in Rembrandt and Frans Hals. Hals was always "true to nature" in a much higher degree than Rembrandt, whose exuberant imagination often allowed him to veil his images in an aura of mystery.

Chapter 1

Learning to construct the head

My students often hear me repeating the time-honored truism: authority in draftsmanship can be achieved only through long practice. The same is not quite true in painting. A good draftsman can be taught to paint well in relatively few lessons. Once the skill of your hand becomes firmly established, theoretical information alone—perhaps just reading—can communicate the principles of oil paint manipulation. But skill in drawing cannot be acquired by reading texts, no matter how well conceived these may be. I remember well the words of my teacher, Max Doerner, in Munich. He used to say: "You can't learn swimming on a sofa." Thus, I do not expect the student to become proficient in drawing just by familiarizing himself with the principles in this treatise. However, it is a fair assumption that the methods developed here will, in some measure, help the student acquire such proficiency.

These methods are not conventional, although I suspect that they are not entirely new either, for nothing as simple, reasonable, and practical could have remained unnoticed by all my predecessors. Now the method I shall discuss—establishing a mnemonic pattern in the mind of the student, a kind of "memory system" for drawing—should create a prototype of every element in the human form. Thus, the reader can refer later to these patterns or prototypes as the need arises. With such *a priori* knowledge, the student may be able to discover aspects in his subject that he would most likely overlook.

Knowing what to look for

It is a common experience that when we behold an object without knowing beforehand what to look for, our image of it is incomplete and often false. To illustrate this, consider the examples in Figs. 1, 2, and 3.

When he looks at the nose of a model, the inexperienced student will usually carry the light over the entire frontal plane (Fig. 1A), not realizing that the light stops at the point where the plane changes its direction to form the nostrils (Fig. 1B).

In Figs. 2A and 2B, although the entire side plane is in shade, it appears that the surface over the nostrils is actually a little lighter. Invariably, the beginner will make this nostril surface just as if it were seen in full light (Fig. 2A), thus creating a confusion in the light and shade relations. This occurs because the student fails to realize that the slight difference in

Plate 1. Lili (The Artist's Wife). *Metropolitan Museum of Art, New York. The rhythmic sequences of the folds—what Goethe called "the manifold echoes of the body's movement"—have been consciously exploited here. Within the geometric design of the background, the paint has been applied with dynamic strokes that swirl around the head.*

tone is due to the insignificant prominence of this surface. In fact, the difference between these shadowy surfaces should be under-emphasized rather than over-emphasized. For one of the important principles of portrait painting is to *minimize all lighter areas* as they appear on the shadow side of the face and, conversely, to *minimize all shadows* on the part of the face turned toward the light.

In the pair of eyes in Fig. 3, it may seem strange that the white of the eye on the shadow side of the face (Fig. 3B) is *lighter* than the white of the eye on the light side of the face (Fig. 3A). To understand this, you have to know that in Fig. 3B the eyelashes are turned away from the light source, thus allowing the light to reach the spherical surface; whereas, in Fig. 3A, the eyelashes cast a shadow on the white of the eye.

I have introduced these examples to illustrate the importance of *a priori* knowledge. The following mnemonic (or memory) patterns, as I call them, will create, in the student's mind, a comprehension of the *basic* forms which underly every particular form. When I call a form *basic*, I mean a *geometric form*; whereas a *particular form* will often deviate, in some manner, from the underlying geometricity. Once this geometric certainty becomes firmly established in your mind, you can assess all particular deviations from the prototype.

Limited study of anatomy

Presently we shall discuss the construction of the head, later the construction of head and shoulders, and so forth. *Construction*, in this instance, is synonymous with anatomy—a forbidding term if we look at books on the subject.

Now anatomy can mean many things to many men. It can be conceived in medical, mythological, classic, or even metaphysical terms. Its study was once thought to be indispensable to the general education of the painter and even the architect. The great Renaissance theoretician of esthetics, Alberti, praised the proportions of the human body as

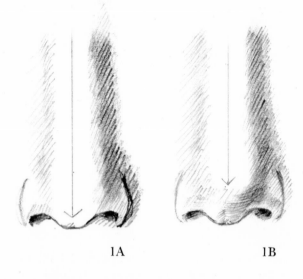

1A   1B

Figure 1. *The inexperienced student will carry the light over the entire frontal plane (1A), not realizing that the light stops at the point where the plane changes direction (1B).*

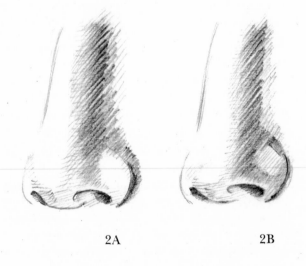

2A   2B

Figure 2. *The patch of light over the nostril form should not be emphasized (2A), but rather de-emphasized (2B) because it appears on the shadow side of the nose.*

14

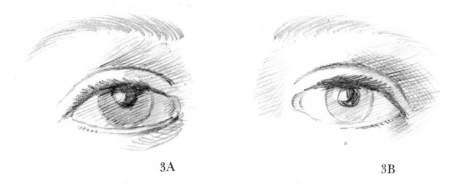

3A
3B

Figure 3. *The white of the eye on the light side of the face (3A) is dimmed by the cast shadow of the lashes. The white of the eye on the dark side of the face (3B) receives more light because the lashes turn away from the light source, thus casting less shadow.*

a visual realization of musical harmony; the leading Roman architect, Vitruvius (1st century, A.D.), suggested identification of human proportions with those of buildings to demonstrate both the "architectural symmetry of the human body and the anthropomorphic vitality of architecture."

I find all this to be a gross exaggeration; besides the element of symmetry, what could the grand plan of the human body have to do with the structure of inanimate objects? When I mention Renaissance man's bias in favor of anatomical knowledge, it must be understood that this discipline meant something else to him than it does to us.

However, familiarity with the mechanism of the body seems essential, whatever its basis: whether *realistic*, faithful to the characteristics of a specific model (as was Rembrandt); or *classical*, true to a preconceived geometric ideal (as was Greek sculpture); or *symbolic*, the art of primitives who seek meaning through symbols. For without some anatomical knowledge, the authenticity of the representation, whatever its nature, will always be questionable.

In my study of many works on artistic anatomy, beginning with Vesalius (16th century), I find that one particular approach has been neglected by past authors: teaching students *mnemonic* patterns—ways of remembering arrangements of light and shade. Granted, it

is quite impressive to see charts which peel off the outer muscles, piece by piece, or to look at a vertebra from all conceivable angles, for this gives us the feeling of being admitted to the inner sanctum of esoteric knowledge.

As a young anatomy student in European art academies, I too had to be conversant with the topography of a *condyle*, or a *maleolus externus*; indeed, we were expected to draw from memory the appearance of a *processus corracoideus*! Now, after having drawn thousands of human bodies, I confess that, today, I am not certain how many vertebrae we have, and I refuse to bow my head in shame because I am even in doubt as to how many of our ribs join the *sternum*.

Bodies often differ to such an extent that what may appear as an anatomical "fact," in one case, may be contradicted in another. Of course, variations in the distribution of fatty tissues, hypertrophy (enlargement), or atrophy (shrinkage) of one muscle strand or another, account for the difference. Yet, to see a definite conformation on *one* body, and to miss it on *another*, can often be quite disconcerting. Here schematization—which we shall consider in the next pages—becomes important. Once we establish a *constant*—a schematic concept of form—against which deviations can be accurately assessed, we shall be better able to avoid confusion.

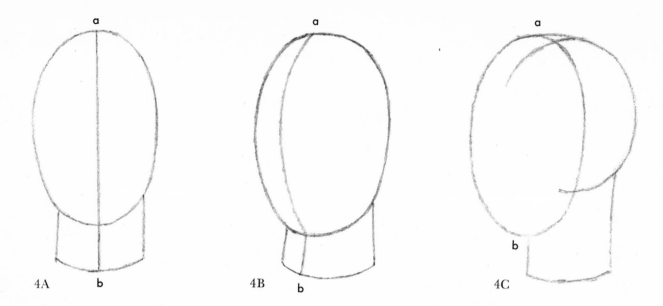

Figure 4A. *Head, divided by the axis, front view. 4B. Three-quarter view. 4C. Seen in profile, the head has an additional shape: a circle is added to the oval to indicate the side view of the skull. Seen in this position, the frontal axis forms the outer contour of the oval.*

Head shape and placement of features

The head comes in many possible shapes; it is easy to verify this. When the head is seen from front and three-quarter views, we may consider an oval as the basic shape. Here, I am thinking of a specific oval, one that would circumscribe a classic head of the Greek prototype. In Fig. 4, this basic oval is divided by the axis (a-b) which separates the features bilaterally. Now, whenever you draw the oval, the next step should be the indication of this axis. Why is this so important? Such a start is imperative because the features will be aligned symmetrically on both sides of the axis. After having drawn tens of thousands of heads, I always start to draw in this manner.

In Fig. 5, the oval is visualized as three-dimensional. The horizontal parallel lines (a-b and c-d) encircling it should be placed at once. The first of these lines (a-b) marks the level of the eyebrows; the second (c-d), the end of the nose; and the third, the mouth. In Fig. 5A, the frontal view, the parallels appear as straight lines, when seen at eye level. In Fig. 5B, the parallels curve because the head

is seen from above. The degree of this curvature depends on the position of the head and the position of the viewer.

In Fig. 6, the head appears in a raised (6A) and bent (6B) position. Here, another important function of the parallels (a-b and c-d) is clearly demonstrated: their distance, one from another, will always encompass the ears.

Head, neck, and shoulders

Now let us add the neck and shoulders to the head (Fig. 7). As we have given the head a simple oval shape, we simplify the neck to a tubular form, and the shoulders to a lozenge. Thus, in Fig. 7A, the neck rests within the

---

Plate 2. Head with Veil. *Collection, E. J. De Witt, Winnetka, Illinois. Veils always glorify a prosaic hairdo and assume a timeless shape that transcends current fashion. Notice how the brush strokes follow the contours of the face. The background darkens at the distant edge of the veil, which blurs into shadow.*

16

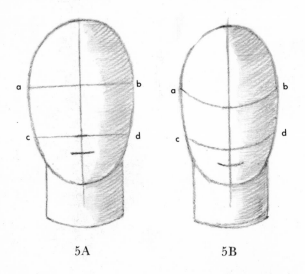

5A   5B

Figure 5A. *Head divided by the axis and parallels; front view, seen at eye level. 5B. Head seen from slightly above.*

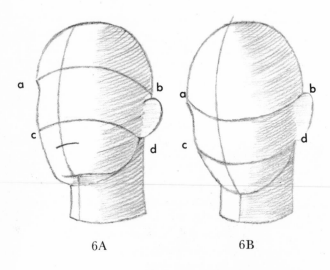

6A   6B

Figure 6A. *Head seen from below. 6B. Head seen from above. Note that the ear always falls between parallels a-b and c-d, whether the head is raised or bent.*

lozenge bordered in front by the *clavicles* (a), and in the back by the *trapezius* (b). In Fig. 7B, the true form of the neck, as it appears in profile, is represented; the area (c) forms a concavity which accommodates the jaw. In Fig. 7C, the head, neck, and shoulders are developed, in addition to the two important muscles—the *sternomastoids* (d-e) that are used in moving the head. These are attached behind the ear (d) to the *mastoid* process on the skull, and terminate between the *clavicles* (e) where the *breastbone* (the *sternum*) forms a slight curve (f). In Fig. 7D, both the head and shoulders are posed in profile.

From the schematic and general, we may now proceed to particulars. In Fig. 7E, the head is turning away, which allows the tendon of the *sternomastoid* to register distinctly at the *sternum* (f). This two-part muscle appears without the overlying skin and, at its termination, it reveals its attachment to both the *sternum* (f) and the *clavicle* (a). However, the muscle strand (g) is visible only on very thin necks and on some aged persons. Such anatomical marks cannot very well be recorded in a portrait as this is apt to displease the patron.

If you suspect that a successful portrait painter must also be a beautician of sorts, alas, you are right. To put it with less cynicism, the portrait artist should certainly be a skilled diplomat. However, since this book is not concerned with such amenities as seeking portrait commissions, we shall quickly return to the technicalities of pictorial anatomy.

To look once more at Fig. 7E and the point marked (h), what *is* this bump, not always in evidence, especially on well upholstered bodies? It is called the *acromium process*, and it is the point where the clavicle (a), curving slightly from the front towards the shoulder, meets the joint of the shoulder blade. Beyond it (h), the arms issue from the shoulder. The muscle (i) covering the joint of the shoulder is called the *deltoid*. With this scheme in mind, we should be able to evaluate what our eye sees and thus correctly render our impression of the model's anatomy.

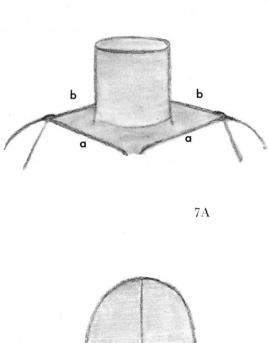

7A

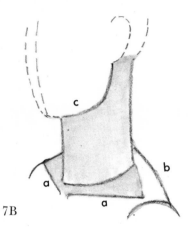

7B

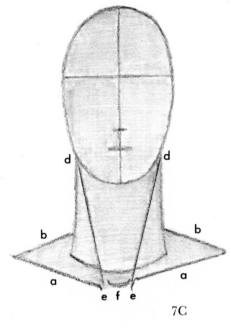

7C

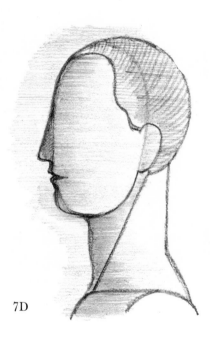

7D

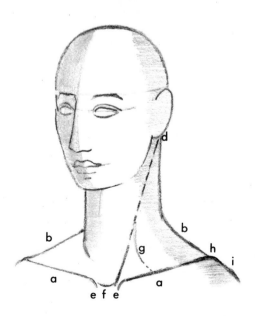

Figure 7A. *Schematic drawing of head and neck, front view. 7B. Neck and shoulders, side view. 7C. Head and neck with sternomastoids added. 7D. Head and shoulders in profile. 7E. Head turned to three-quarter view. Anatomical features: (a) clavicle; (b) trapezius; (c) jaw; (d-e) sternomastoid; (f) breastbone or sternum; (g) strand of sternomastoid; (h) acromium process; (i) deltoid.*

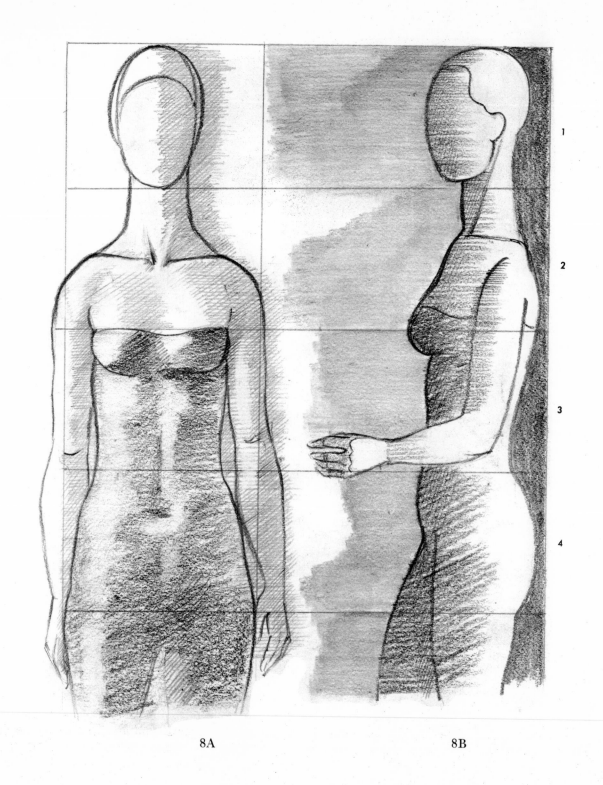

8A

8B

Figure 8. *Approximate proportions of an "ideal" figure which would be 7½ heads high from crown to toe. 8A. Front view of head and torso. 8B. Side view of head and torso.*

Chapter 2

Learning to construct the figure

When we limit ourselves to the head and shoulders, we can consider only three basic positions: front, three-quarter, and profile. However, as soon as we are confronted with the half figure—or a full figure—problems multiply. When the trunk and arms appear on the scene, endless variations of movement arise; consequently, we shall have to draw upon a much larger store of anatomical knowledge.

But since portraits in the nude are uncommon (except with our avant-garde, so called, where shock value is the mainstay of "artistry"), we shall not be concerned with the catalogue of trunk muscles; only arms and legs will have to be dealt with "clinically," so to speak.

Of course, there will be a pressing need to familiarize yourself with hands, which, as every painter knows, pose a number of drawing problems.

Figure proportions

To begin with the basic proportions, these are represented in Fig. 8 in a more than ideal fashion. We may ask, what is *ideal*? The Grecian prototype (Periclean period, 5th century) would be the proper answer, but these ideal measurements call for a slightly short figure in which the total length, head to toe, is 7½ heads. Considering our esthetic preference for a longer body (these cannot really be looked

upon as modern), a length of up to 8½ heads could be chosen without causing undue distortions.

Thus, in Fig. 8, the distance from the chin to the middle of the breast is one head, and the distance from this point to the navel is 1⅓ heads. The elbow hinge reaches just above the navel, and the fingertips—hanging down—touch about the middle of the thighs.

Arms

The muscles of the arms (Fig. 9) are considered next—very briefly, because these will register in their total mass only. As a matter of fact, thus far we have identified only two differentiated muscles: the *sternomastoid* and the *deltoid* (a). The latter starts at the end of the *clavicle* (b) and wraps itself around the side of the *biceps* (c). All of these, as well as the group of muscles in the forearm, will remain unidentified as separate entities; the portrait painter will never be embarrassed by his ignorance of such clinical data.

The interesting—and important—observation that should be made here is that the positions of the two thin bones (the *ulna* forming the elbow, and the *radius*) shape the forearm characteristically. In the position called *pronation* (Fig. 10A), the bones cross one another; here the thumb is directed toward the body. When the thumb points away from the body (*supination*), the bones are in parallel position (Fig. 10B).

Legs

Next we move on to the legs, schematically represented in Fig. 11. You may wonder what place the legs take in contemporary portraiture. Despite current fashion, would you paint a portrait of a lady in tights? Also, gentlemen are not attired in knee breeches à la Gainsborough. In short, although we rarely have an occasion to deal with legs, we should begin a study of anatomy by going straight from head to foot.

Hence, in Fig. 11A, the frontal view reveals the anatomical construction carried out along classic (in this case, Renaissance) doctrines. Now let us analyze the total line a-b-c, the scaffold of the entire structure. In the area a-b, the line divides the inside of the thigh into two gentle curves. Here, a thin, outwardly invisible muscle called *sartorius* (the "tailor" muscle in English) has, to all appearances, only one task: to tie up, as a string does a package, the muscles of the thigh.

In the area of the knee (b-c) the contour line changes its course to the left; below, it again moves slightly to the right. In short, a straight leg is not built around a straight axis! Note the broken axis line in Figs. 11A and 11C. The posterior view (Fig. 11B) reveals a certain symmetry, except for the fact that the bulge of the outer calf is placed higher than the corresponding bulge of the inner calf. The ankle, on the other hand, shows a slant in the opposite direction: the position of the inner ankle is higher than that of the outer side. Only on a flat foot are both ankles perfectly aligned.

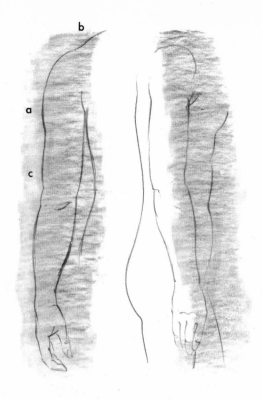

9A   9B

Figure 9A. *Front view of arm. 9B. Side view of arm. The deltoid (a) starts at the end of the clavicle (b) and wraps around the side of the biceps (c)*

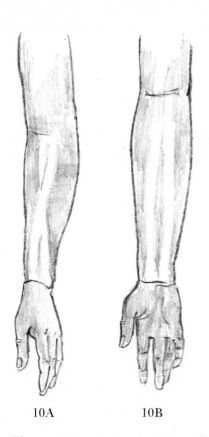

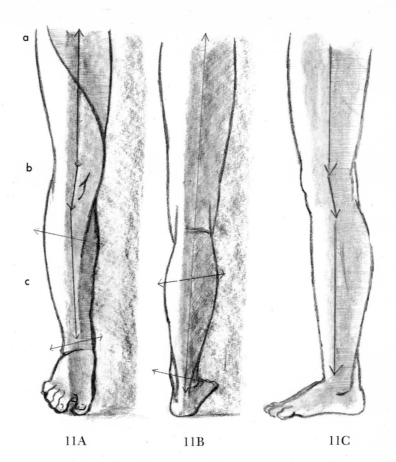

10A   10B   11A   11B   11C

Figure 10A. *In the position called*
pronation, *the bones of the forearm*
cross one another. 10B. In the
position called supination, *the bones*
of the forearm are parallel.

Figure 11A. *Front view of leg.*
Note how line a-b-c divides the
thigh, swings around the knee, then
begins to divide the lower leg. The
vertical axis of the leg is not quite
perpendicular and breaks at the
knee. 11B. Back view of leg. The
axis is unbroken, but note the
relationship of inner and outer
calf muscle and ankle bulges. Study
these same relationships in the
frontal view of the leg (see arrows).
11C. Side view of leg. Once again,
note the broken axis line.

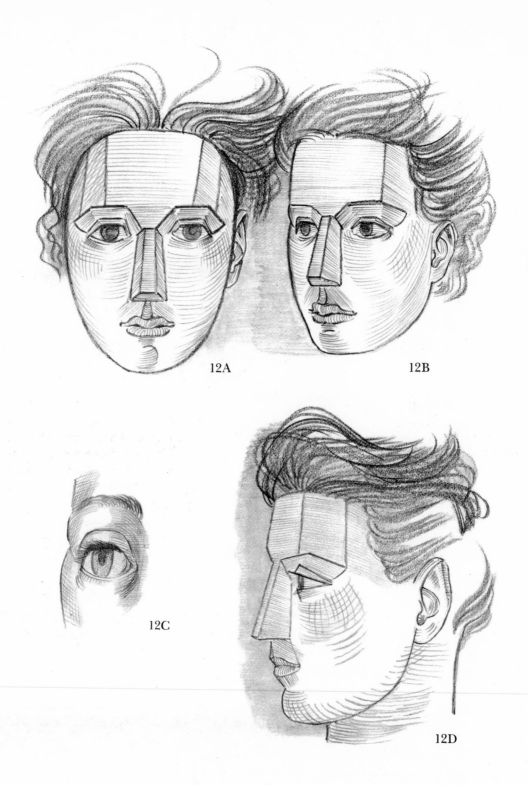

12A

12B

12C

12D

Figure 12. *Geometric representation of face and features. 12A. Front view. 12B. Three-quarter view shows the far side of the face foreshortened. 12C. Detail of 12B shows that the foreshortened eye still remains within the contour of the face, never touching the edge. 12D. Profile view.*

Chapter 3

Facial features

In the foregoing chapter, we discussed some of the anatomical properties of the human figure in general terms. Now we shall consider the head — the proper domain of the portrait painter—more closely, and try to establish a mnemonic pattern of the features (Fig. 12). These features have been geometricized in Fig. 12 because only a *geometric* form is constant; the *particular* form varies.

Of course, in life, features are never symmetrically aligned; one side of the face always differs in some degree from the other side. This can be verified when you look at another person's face in the mirror.

Fig. 12 shows that the three-quarter position (Fig. 12B) displays much greater foreshortening in the part of the face turned away from the viewer. Observe closely the detail in Fig. 12C. Here, the inexperienced will always make the same mistake: he will push the eye socket to the very edge of the face, instead of leaving it contained within the contour, thus allowing the foreshortened cheekbone to register.

Eyes

The eye socket has the shape of a lozenge. The eyelids are symmetrically arranged, more or less, while the eyeball is spherical; that is, its surface is curving, not straight, as the curving arrow indicates (Fig. 13A). The iris, when seen from the front, is perfectly round (Fig.

13A); but from the three-quarter view (Fig. 13B), the iris is oval. From the side view (Fig. 13C), it appears almost as a straight vertical line.

Both eyes are also symmetrically arranged— or almost so. The eyebrows form a low or a high arch above the eyelids and the distance between the eyes can be great or small. All these details must be carefully evaluated when you examine a particular physiognomy.

Nose

First, let us consider the geometric shapes of the nose (Fig. 14). All views are seen from eye level; since the under part of the nose is visible from this view, its shape must be slightly upturned.

The higher the model, and the lower the viewer's eye level, the less will the under part of the nose be foreshortened. Conversely, the higher the position of the viewer, the more the nose will be turned down. Looking at the model from above is always an unfavorable angle of visualization since it foreshortens the length of the neck. In portrait painting, the model should be placed higher than the viewer.

A detail that is often neglected by the inexperienced is the design of the nostrils (Fig. 14D). They are not mere round holes drilled into a flat surface but, as seen in the drawing, complex convoluted shapes.

13A

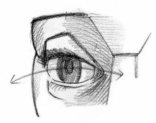

13B

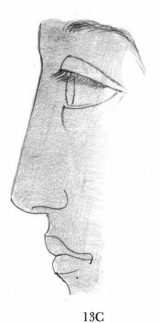

13C

Figure 13A. *Schematic front view of eye shows the eyeball as spherical, indicated by curving arrow.*
13B. Here the eye appears in a fore-shortened position; observe the change in the shape of the iris to an oval. 13C. Seen from the side, the foreshortening is even more pronounced and the iris appears as almost a straight vertical line.

Mouth

Here we have arrived at our most ornamental design—the mouth. Thus, in Fig. 15A, we see the elegant curves of the frontal view, in the Greek style; in Fig. 15B, the three-quarter view; in Fig. 15C, an upturned view; and the position seen from below, in Fig. 15D.

Thus, the "ideal" mouth is shaped like Amor's bow. However, more often than not, nature does not follow Hellenistic notions of beauty—like a deftly manipulated lipstick. Hence, the contours of the mouth may be more or less flat, and the thickness of the upper and lower lips may be at variance with the theoretical ideal.

Ear

Of all the intricate forms found in the human countenance, none is as complicated as the ear. Having only a cursory acquaintance with anthropology, I cannot even conjecture why this should be so. (I am not sure that it makes us hear better.) But, indubitably, it always poses a problem for most painters.

As usual, we shall start with a prototype; however, in this instance, the typical ear I draw will be—my own! It is a fact that in painting ears, many painters have their own in mind, perhaps because this is the most accessible model. (Often, in authenticating old masters' paintings, one of the leads investigated is the manner in which the ears are conceived; incidentally, the same can be said of hands.) Because of the complexity of the structure, a step-by-step procedure in drawing the ear will be needed, as developed in Fig. 16.

Most ears show structures not always identical with the prototype, but the principal difference will be found in the appearance of the *helix* (or outer rim) and the *lobe*. The helix can be flat, or show a ridge terminating halfway down to the lobe or reaching it. The lobe can joint the jaw in a shallow or a deep curve. Moreover, the shape and size of the *concha* (the opening) will vary with different ears. In addition, an ear can hug the skull or protrude in varying degrees.

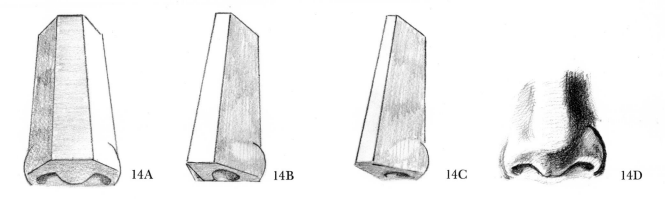

14A   14B   14C   14D

Figure 14A, B, C. *Three geometric views of the nose as seen from eye level. 14D. The nostrils are not mere round holes, but complex curving shapes which demand careful observation.*

15A   15B   15C   15D

Figure 15A. *Front view of lips at eye level. 15B. Three-quarter view of lips at eye level. 15C. Slightly upturned view of lips. 15D. Slightly downturned view of lips.*

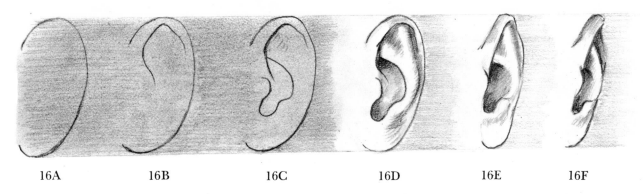

16A   16B   16C   16D   16E   16F

Figure 16A, B, C, and D. *Steps in drawing the ear, beginning with the outline of the over-all shape, moving on to the internal shapes, then concluding with the modeling of the forms. 16E. Partially foreshortened view as the head turns. 16F. Further foreshortening occurs as the head turns from a profile view toward a frontal view.*

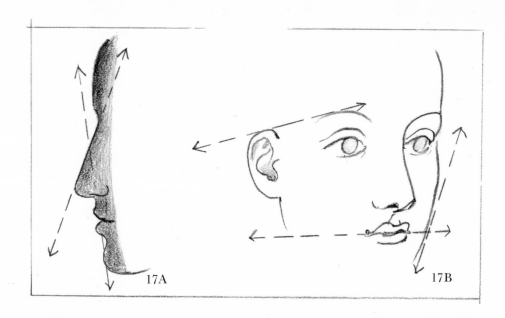

17A   17B

Figure 17A. *In a profile, the variable directional lines or pitch of the nose, lips, and chin are best visualized against an imaginary vertical line. 17B. In the same way, the construction lines of a three-quarter view—the line of the mouth or cheek, the relationship of ear to eye socket—can be gauged against imaginary horizontals and verticals. The construction lines in the drawings are diagonals whose angles were determined by mental comparison with imaginary vertical and horizontal axes.*

Figure 18. *Here horizontal and vertical lines are used to determine the relationships of the features. In this particular view of the head, the inner corner of one eye aligns vertically with the center of the chin, the lower edge of the nose aligns horizontally with the jaw corner, etc. Of course, a slight change in the angle of the head will demolish these relationships and establish new ones. There is no formula. For each head you draw, you must observe new relationships and establish new plumb lines. This method will give you a very accurate idea of the individual proportions of your model in a given view.*

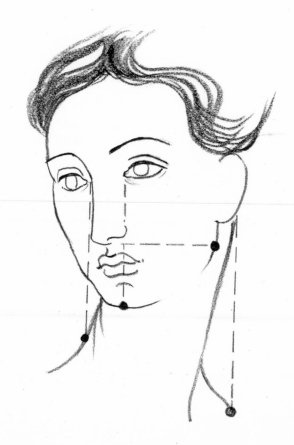

Chapter 4

Aids in getting a likeness

I mentioned that skill in drawing can be attained only through constant practice. Now I am suggesting *aids* to facilitate your progress, which may sound like a contradiction of my former statement. However, the suggested aids have only one purpose; to help you register the observed facts more accurately.

One age-old device is particularly useful: gauging all the variable directional lines of the model's features (or figure) against two constants: *a vertical and a horizontal line*.

The "constants" are rather abstractly conceived, since they are not materially present, but purely imaginary—in your mind's eye. The painter may resort to his brush, holding it first vertically, then horizontally, thus gauging the deviations (from horizontal or vertical) of the salient elements in his subject.

Vertical and horizontal guidelines

Consider a profile and a three-quarter view (Fig. 17). When we establish vertical and horizontal lines (in the mind's eye), we can then assess all lines deviating from these constants.

Another way of measuring the position of a feature is to project (that is, to plumb) one of its salient points to another feature, thus establishing their relative placement. This process is demonstrated in Fig. 18.

Studying Fig. 18, you will see that vertical lines have been drawn to establish the placement of one eye corner in relation to the nostril wing and chin, the placement of the other eye corner in relation to the lower curve of the cheek and to the concavity where neck joins shoulder, etc. A horizontal line relates the root of the nose to the jaw corner. Obviously, all these relationships will change with the slightest shift of the head and new vertical and horizontal lines must be drawn to record the new relationships.

Observing general character of head

The aids I have described concern *general* measurements. What about *specific* characteristics that account for a likeness?

Here we can proceed as follows. First observe the general character of the head; it can fall into the category of a round or oval shape (Fig. 19). Next, study the features, the forehead—high or low; the nose—short or long; and the distance between the nose and the mouth. Next, note the slant of the eyes (Fig. 20), and the shape of the nose (Fig. 21). All these are initial observations which you should make carefully *before* you begin to work.

Besides observing physiognomical proportions, you must also observe the coloristic appearance of the sitter's hair and complexion. These contribute — sometimes moderately, sometimes greatly—to the characteristics that account for a likeness.

29

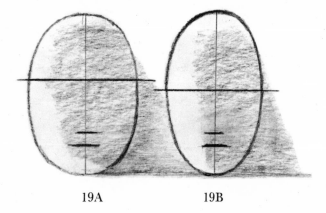

19A 19B

Figure 19. *In studying the sitter to establish a likeness, you must first observe the general character of the head. Is it round (19A) or oval (19B)? Is the forehead high (19B) or low (19A)? Is the distance between brow and the root of the nose relatively great (19A) or somewhat less (19B)?*

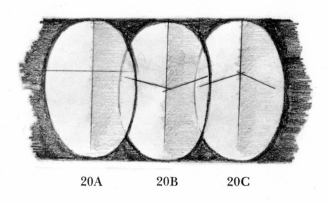

20A 20B 20C

Figure 20. *Examine the slant of the eyes. Are they level (20A), upward slanting (20B), or downward slanting(20C)?*

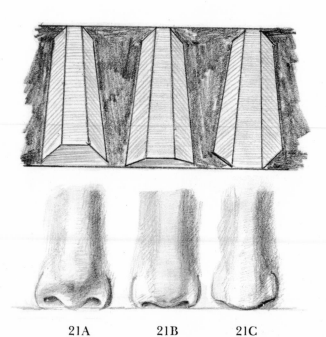

21A 21B 21C

Figure 21. *Study the shape of the nose. Does it tend to turn up (21A), is it fairly level (21B), or does it tend to turn down(20C)?*

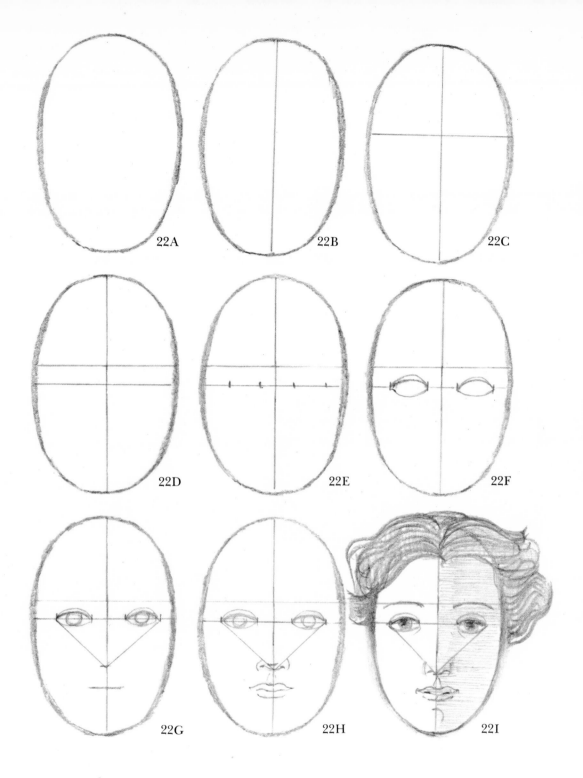

Figure 22. *Steps to achieve a likeness. 22A. Draw an oval of the correct shape for the sitter's head. 22B. Draw a vertical axis. 22C. Draw the horizontal line of the eyebrows. 22D. Draw the horizontal line of the eyes. 22E. Indicate the length of the eyes. 22F. Place the eyes and draw their contours. 22G. Draw a triangle between the corners of the eyes and the root of the nose, plus the line of the mouth. 22H. Draw the shape of the nose and mouth. 22I. Indicate the forehead and hair.*

A method for getting a likeness

Some artists have a gift for achieving a likeness and proceed without effort and without any special devices. However, this faculty is not possessed by many—not by your author, who, in spite of long and wide experience in the field of portraiture, still adheres to the procedures which he developed many years ago, shown in Fig. 22.

To proceed step by step, start with a generalized shape of the head—that is, a simple, nonspecific shape—a narrow or a wider oval that characterizes the particular model you are drawing. Next, the bilateral vertical division of the head—whether the head is seen from front or side—indicated by a vertical line. Then add the horizontal at the height of the eyebrows, and the line connecting the eye corners. On this eye horizontal, mark the space between the eyes with dots, plus the width of the eyes (the outer corners).

Now the length of the nose will emerge if you draw lines that connect the outer limits of the eyes with the root of the nose; these lines will form a triangle. Depending on the width of the eye-line and the length of the nose, the triangle can be steep or shallow, in varying degrees. Thus, the nature of this triangle is one of the most significant physiognomical characteristics. When this is done, the distance between the root of the nose and the mouth, and the distance between mouth and chin, will be arrived at without much search.

The importance of the device seen in Fig. 22G (and shown separately in Fig. 23) lies in the fact that the main characteristic of a group of features—for practicing portraitists—is inherent in the *relationships* of the features, not merely in the features themselves.

One more observation concerning the contour of the face, as it appears in Fig. 24. After the features have been placed in their proper position, this contour will precisely follow the predetermined pattern. It will accommodate the forehead, eyesockets, cheekbones, and so forth, thus minimizing the chance of error.

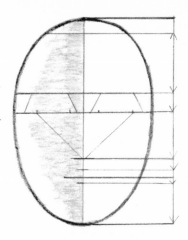

Figure 23. *Here are the schematic lines of the method shown step by step in Fig. 22.*

Figure 24. *When the features have been placed in their correct position within the grid in Fig. 23, you will find that all features fall into their proper places.*

Plate 3. Boy in Yellow Jacket. *Private collection. Portraits need not be formally posed. They can just be "pictures." Study the pattern of light and shade on the head and refer to the mnemonic patterns in Chapter 7.*

34

Chapter 5

Positions of head, neck, and shoulders

I mentioned that, in portraiture, discretion should be our guiding principle. This means that anything extravagant, such as an affected or forced pose, should be avoided. Undue animation—broad smiles, flashing teeth, snapshot attitudes, pretentious or artificial stances —all these will taint the portrait with sham and make it vulgar or commonplace.

Therefore, when you plan a painting that includes no more than the head and shoulders, the pose should be simple, since movements (other than the turn of the head) do not appear. For these movements, our choice will be limited to those shown in Figs. 25, 26, and 27.

Whatever positions we allow the head to assume (full face, three-quarters, profile), and whether the sitter is turned to the right or left, will all depend on what appears to be a more favorable view of the particular sitter.

In the foregoing examples, we have exhausted most of the angles from which head and shoulders can be observed while we maintain our position slightly below the eye level of the model—the most advantageous point of visualization in portrait painting, as I said earlier.

Plate 4. Mrs. Orson Munn. *Do I have a penchant for capes? Like veils and turbans, these will remain in good taste forever. Note how the lights emerge from the background and how the shadows melt into the surrounding dark tones.*

Body in front view

In Fig. 25A, the frontal view is represented. When the head and figure are turned in one direction, they appear static, and animation would come only when the eyes of the model turn sideways. Such static, frontal views are characteristic of early Renaissance portraiture.

In Fig. 25B, the head is turned to the side, which gives a more animated appearance, especially when the gaze of the model is directed toward the beholder. In this position, the tendon of the sternomastoid articulates more clearly, thus enlivening the column of the neck.

In Fig. 25C, the strain of the sternomastoid is greatly intensified; in fact, this muscle appears here at its fullest extension, giving the head a somewhat uncomfortable position in its sudden thrust. However, a young model with a long neck would justify such a pose.

Body diagonal to picture plane

In all the poses in Fig. 26, the body is turned so that it is diagonal to the picture plane. In the foregoing example, it was parallel. The result of this position is greater animation, especially in Fig. 26A, where the body and the head turn in different directions. In this particular position, the axis of the head is slightly tilted, in keeping with the naturalness of the pose.

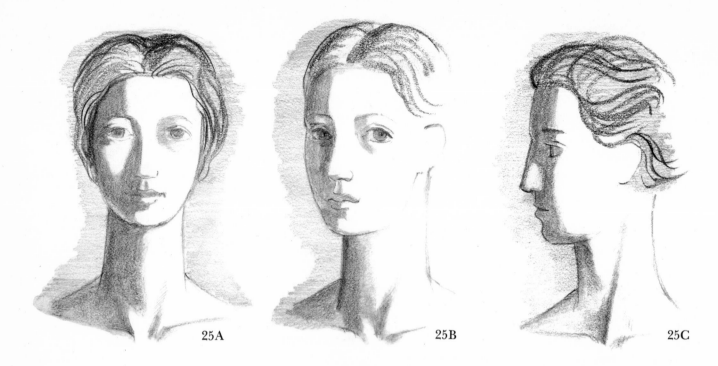

Figure 25.   *In these three poses, the body faces the artist while head and neck turn. 25A. Head and neck face directly forward. 25B. Three-quarter view of head and neck. 25C. Head and neck face to the side, but the shoulders are seen from the front.*

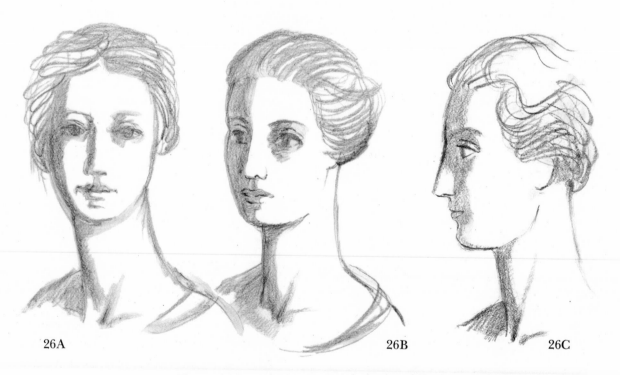

Figure 26A.   *The head faces the artist while the neck and shoulders turn toward a three-quarter position. 26B. Head, neck, and shoulders all turn to a three-quarter position. 26C. Head and neck are seen in profile, while the shoulders are turned to a three-quarter position.*

36

Figure 27. *In all three of these poses, the body is seen virtually in profile, while the head faces the artist (27A), turns to a three-quarter view (27B), and finally turns to a profile view (27C).*

In Fig. 26B, where head and body assume the same direction, this static position suggests a mood of serenity and detachment, especially when the model's gaze is turned away from the viewer. Whether this pose is more advantageous than the one seen in Fig. 26A depends on the character and type of the model, which ultimately dictates its pictorialization.

In Fig. 26C, the head is seen in profile. If this view of the sitter's head is selected—a decision suggested by the appearance of the sitter—a pose in which head and body take different directions is most effective, as a rule.

Body in profile

In Fig. 27, the body is seen almost in profile. Again, in Fig. 27A, the severe turn of the slightly bent head (corresponding to the natural response of the neck's muscles) allows the head to face the beholder squarely. The dynamic movement is stronger here than in any other pose, except perhaps in Fig. 25C. These stark contrasts between the position of the head and the body can be considered only when the length of the neck and the youthful age of the model allow such a pose. Of course, I am thinking here of a female model only, when a "poetic" mood seems proper to the occasion.

In Fig. 27B, the pose is more natural and much easier for the model to maintain without strain. In the previous illustration (Fig. 27A), the model could pose only for short periods at a time. When a three-quarter view of the face is chosen, the relation of the head and body seems to be most favorable, since it is less static than the ones represented in Fig. 25A and Fig. 25B.

But the most static of all the poses—conforming to the ideal of the early Renaissance masters—is the profile view, Fig. 27C. The conception of a profile is more sculpturesque than any of our other examples, except perhaps Fig. 25A. The profile is an *inherently* sculptural pose.

Chapter 6

Half, three-quarter, and full figures

Early in this century (or perhaps much earlier) there was one measuring method generally taught in art schools: the artist measured the proportions of features with a pencil or a stick of charcoal held in his hand, which was stretched out at arm's length, while he stood at an easel, a good distance from the model. Thus he measured, for example, the relative length of the nose, marking its size by holding a thumbnail at the appropriate point on the measuring stick. Then, according to his fancy, he would plumb the size of, say, the nose in the total length of the head, and arrive at a certain ratio. Sound as such a method is, it cannot work on small measurements.

However, when we deal with a *figure*, we shall use such a plumbing method advantageously to establish the correct proportions between head, body, and limbs—as well as to find the positions of parts of the body—while we decide on an animated pose (as opposed to a static one). Of course, for further control, our constants—the vertical and horizontal lines —will always be fixed in our mind's eye (study the example in Fig. 28).

Plate 5.   Boy in Blue (The Artist's Son). *San Diego City Fine Arts Gallery. A slight hint of the outdoors—a few landscape elements, some plants in the background, etc.—can be timeless and unpretentious.*

Placing figure in picture space

Before discussing the problems connected with painting more than the sitter's head and shoulders, let me emphasize that the placement of the figure on the canvas is an important matter to decide. To start with the *unfavorable* divisions, first let us examine Figs. 30A, 31A, 32A, and 33A.

In Fig. 30A, the design of the figure terminates right under the breast. Terminating just above the breast (Fig. 30B) is better.

In Fig. 31A, short, inconclusive fragments of the upper arm appear. However, should such fragments be covered by a dress, the cut-off would not be objectionable. One might also include the full arm, which actually frames and stabilizes the composition in Fig. 31B.

In Figs. 32A and 33A, another optical phenomenon enters when a figure (or any other object) reaches to the bottom bar of the frame: our gaze does not end at the frame, but continues on its course downward, conjuring up the existence of the object *beyond* its limits.

In Fig. 33A, the legs of the sitter appear to stretch ad infinitum. Likewise, in Fig. 32A, the width of the hips may, in our inner eye, expand unduly; besides, the figure ends at the crotch—a very bad termination.

In Fig. 32A, both arms terminate at the joint—an inappropriate point. Whether directly at the elbow, wrist, knee, or ankle—or

39

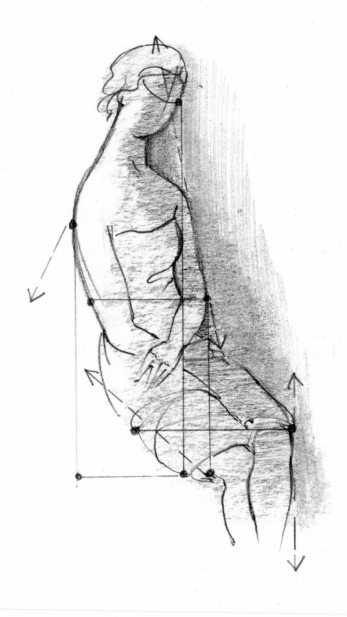

Figure 28. *Here the plumb line method originally applied to the head—establishing imaginary lines to determine the relationships of various elements in the drawing—is applied to the figure.*

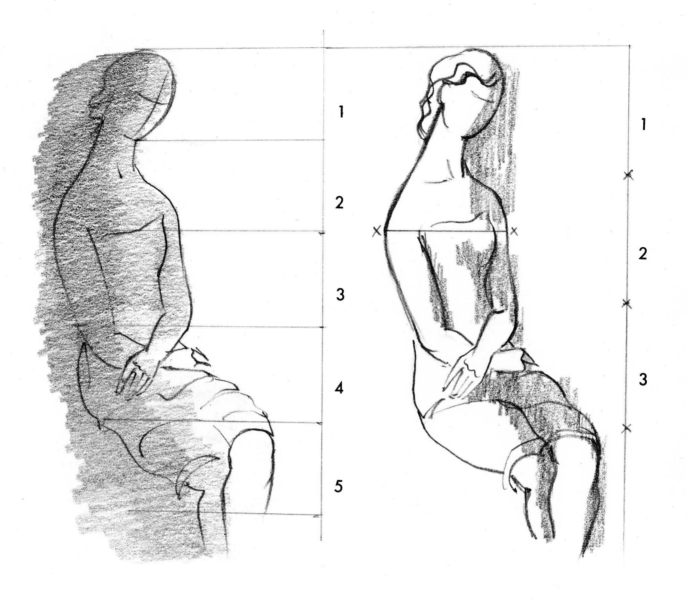

Figure 29. *Here we establish the proportions of the figure by relating all proportions to the length of the head. Thus, the distance from chin to center of chest is one head (in this pose), from chest to elbow is roughly one head (in this pose), etc. Naturally, the proportions will reflect not only the pose, but the shape of the sitter, and the purposeful distortions of the artist.*

30A   30B

Figure 30A. *This is an example of unfortunate placement of the figure within the rectangle of the canvas or panel. The figure is chopped off at the bottom of the breast, which rests uncomfortably on the bottom edge of the rectangle. 30B. It is better to terminate slightly above the breast.*

 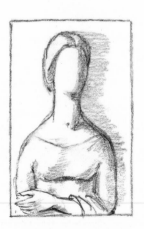

31A   31B

Figure 31A. *Equally bad, the figure is chopped off just above the elbow, leaving inconclusive fragments of the upper arm.*
31B. Actually including the arm will frame and stabilize the composition by adding a strong horizontal at the base.

slightly above or below—such truncations will always be unpleasant to the eye. We can make it a basic rule that a limb shall not end at its joint. In the same example (Fig. 32A), the three-quarter length of the figure terminates at the hip joint—decidedly an unfavorable position. But when we end the figure slightly above the hip, or at about the middle of the thighs, the design of the figure will be pleasing. Or we can save Fig. 32A by including both arms in a rhythmic arrangement that overlaps the hips (Fig. 32B).

In Fig. 33A, the sitter is seen almost full length; regardless of how the male or female sitter is dressed, cutting off the feet makes a bad termination. It is better to include the entire figure (Fig. 33B).

When arms and hands appear in a picture, the painter's problems will multiply. But in the realm of portraiture, where simplicity will be our guiding principle, there are surprisingly few poses which a model can assume with impunity—that is, without displaying poor taste.

Treatments of hands

Should you master all the problems that may have arisen thus far, the difficulty that you face next is a major one: the treatment of hands. Why should painting hands present special difficulties? While it is hard to tell, it would seem that the principal reason lies in their enormous mobility, resulting in an endless variety of positions. And how many students will devote their attention to the serious study of hands? Although a student may make a hundred sketches from a model's head, few will attempt even ten drawings of hands.

There can be no mistake about it: mastery of hands—either in drawing or painting—is not easily attained. When he paints a commissioned portrait, every painter undoubtedly knows that his study of the sitter's hands will be put under a severe handicap. Even if the sitter is patient when he poses for his head, his patience often evaporates by the time the artist is ready to paint hands.

When you study hands in portraits by the

old masters, it becomes apparent at once that most of these hands were painted from a model who was not the sitter. Using such a substitute, the painter could finish his work in a more relaxed mood, without having to contend with his client's impatience or with his inability to maintain a pose.

Four rules for painting hands

When you paint hands, a few general rules should be observed:

(1) Do not view hands in extreme foreshortening; these poses are very difficult to handle.

(2) Do not paint only a small segment of the hand because, when seen as a fragment, it will not explain itself; the hand will not articulate.

(3) Try to obtain a light and shade relationship on the hand which will clarify its structure. This structure will be more expressive when you divide the hand into distinct light and shade areas: one extending from the wrist to the knuckles, the other from the knuckles to the fingertips (Fig. 34B).

(4) Do not paint the hand with a perfect finish, that is, in meticulous detail.

The hints and suggestions given above may appear to be arbitrary strictures dictated by my particular bias. However, this is not the case; should you, reader, now interject and say that greatly detailed hands are found in the work of some of the great old masters, this does not give us license to follow suit; for the esthetic that legislates the art of portraiture in *our* day is different from the one that was followed by some of the ancient schools.

Regarding sketchiness of execution, we can learn a lesson from paintings by Frans Hals, whose power in the treatment of hands remains unmatched. Although, occasionally, he may have carried out a face in great detail without the customary bravura, the hands are almost always dashed off in a sketchy manner. But whenever they appear tight and labored, his hands are much less expressive than those treated casually. However, do not conclude

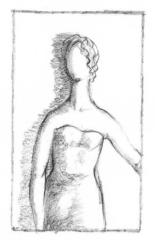 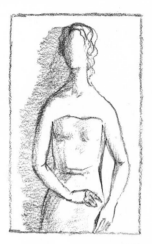

32A   32B

Figure 32A. *In this awkward placement of the figure on the canvas, one arm is chopped off at the elbow, while the other is chopped off at the wrist. The torso, itself, ends at the hip joint, which is equally unfortunate. 32B. Here the arms are added in full, composed in a rhythmic arrangement which overlaps the hips, minimizing the effect of the hip joint cut-off.*

33A   33B

Figure 33A. *In a full length figure, cutting off the feet is always a mistake, regardless of how the sitter is dressed. 33B. It is wisest to include the entire figure.*

43

Plate 6.   Portrait Study. *Private collection. The relaxed, unconventional pose takes the picture out of the realm of "posed" formal portraiture. Flowers are a charming prop, enhancing the feminine subject.*

44

that we could readily adopt Frans Hals' style of painting; the naturalism of his representation would never convey the same meaning today as it did in the 17th century.

To return to hands, vitality is their prime characteristic—conveyed by the never-ending play and animation of the fingers and their changing positions (Fig. 34). It is the positions of the fingers and their interrelationships that should be carefully considered when you design hands. It is *not* arbitrary whether this or that finger appears separated from the rest, or whether they are held tightly together, bent, or outstretched. Generally, it is the position of the arm and the pose of the model that will suggest the arrangement of the fingers.

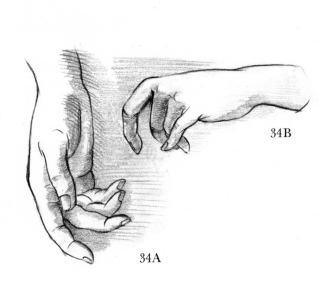

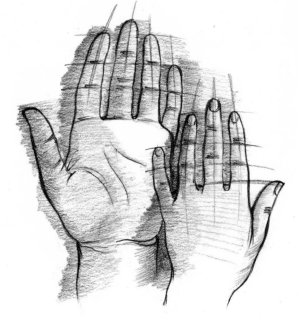

Figure 34A. *It is important to paint the entire hand—not isolated fragments of hands—avoiding extreme foreshortening. Simplify the forms and eliminate detail; there is no need to render every wrinkle. 34B. It is best to divide the hand into two basic areas of light and shade. Here, the light extends from wrist to knuckles; the fingers, below the knuckles, are predominantly in shadow.*

Figure 35. *In constructing the hand, it is helpful to visualize lines that run through the joints. However, note that the joints do not align precisely; for example, study the relationship of the little finger to the adjacent finger. It is also useful to visualize axis lines running the length of each finger; note that these axes curve inward toward one another.*

46

Chapter 7

Patterns of light and shade

Some time ago, after teaching art for nearly thirty years, I conceived a method of studying the drawing of a head that seemed strange at first, but which, over the course of years, proved eminently successful. The idea behind the method is a simple one: namely, to make the student prefigure in his mind—in the absence of a model—the plastic or three-dimensional appearance of the features. As we know, only light and shade show plasticity of form and thus explain its nature.

Mouth and chin

Consider, for example, a three-quarter view of the mouth and chin, as seen in normal studio light, Fig. 36. What does the pattern of light and shade indicate?

First, it shows clearly that one side of the face (a) is turned toward the light and receives its full impact. But the other side (b) is turned slightly away from the light; thus it will be in half shadow. The hollow between

Plate 7. Fred Nagler. *Collection, Encyclopedia Britannica, Chicago, Illinois. It is a real joy to face a model who can assume a professional attitude while posing. The sitter is an artist, of course, and a symbol of his trade makes an effective background. A brush makes a handy prop for him to hold, and he wears the classic smock.*

nose and lips (c) will be in shade at the edge of the hollow adjoining the area of light, but it will be seen in full light as it curves upward. An analogous situation arises on the surface of the curving lower lip (d): the left side will receive a highlight; there will be in shade on the right side. Because the surface under the lower lip (e) is indented, it will be partially in shade; but the protruding chin (f) will catch the light, forming a characteristic pattern which is apparent on every model's face.

Now let us turn to Fig. 37, the drawing of a mouth. Why is the upper lip's surface (a) always dark and the lower lip's surface (b) always light when seen in normal studio light coming from the front? The directional lines (c and d), indicating the angles of the surfaces, explain this. It is obvious that the upper lip's surface (a) could be light only if it were illuminated from below, perhaps by footlights as seen on a stage.

Light and shadow on head

All the effects described above seem evident at first glance. But judging from many students' responses, these points often are not obvious. The student may face a model and still fail to realize the nature of the underlying form that accounts for the particular interdependence of the areas of light and shade. Therefore, I endeavor to make the student understand the

47

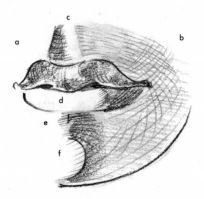

Figure 36. *One side of the face (a) turns to the light, while the other (b) turns slightly away from the light and is in half shadow. The hollow above the lips (c) is in shadow at the edge that adjoins the light area (a), but picks up the light as it curves forward, adjoining shadow area (b). In the same way, the lower lip (d), the surface beneath the lower lip (e), and the chin (f) have light and shadow sides. This characteristic pattern appears on virtually every model's face under normal studio lighting conditions.*

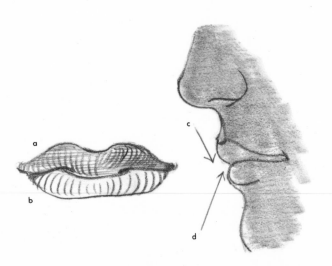

Figure 37. *Under normal studio lighting conditions, the upper lip (a) is angled downward (c) and is therefore in shadow, while the lower lip (b) turns up (d) and catches the light.*

inevitable logic of the light and shade relationship, to establish in his mind an *a priori* certainty or a *constant* against which he may gauge all the variables, as they appear with so many different models. Thus, a standard (mnemonic) pattern is established in the student's memory; hence his margin of error will be greatly reduced.

Such mnemonic patterns are seen in Figs. 38, 39, and 40. In order to make them more distinct, the shadow areas are not blended with the areas of the light; half shadows are marked by lines.

What is the significance of these patterns of light and shade, one might ask? The answer is simple. In Figs. 38B, 39B, and 40B, the plasticity of the head, because of the increase in the shadow area, is greatly enhanced. We can say that here the chiaroscuro is more dramatic than in Figs. 38A, 39A, and 40A. Is this always an advantage? Not necessarily. It all depends on the type of model. On young faces—especially those of females—the preponderance of *light* and the reduction of shadows is, as a rule, more advantageous.

Favorable and unfavorable lighting

In the foregoing section, I discussed patterns of light and shade that are sometimes favorable in painting a portrait and sometimes less so—all depending on the difficulties involved in handling a particular painting. What is good lighting? And is there a manner of lighting that we should avoid?

Let us look at the beginning of photographic portraiture, developed by Daguerre before the middle of the 19th century, and known as Daguerreotype. Those early photographic portraits are distinguished by a beauty that has never been recaptured. What is the virtue that explains the charm of these photographs? The answer is: conformity to the simple, classic precepts of chiaroscuro, which called for the use of only *one source of light.*

In classic portraiture, as a rule, light entered through a side window, generally on the painter's left. When we behold these portraits,

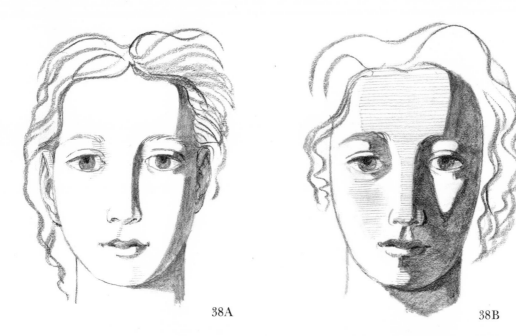

38A   38B

Figure 38A.   *Here the head is seen in full view, with almost the entire surface
in light and only a narrow pattern of shadows. 38B. As the light moves more
to the side, a wider pattern of shadows—and half shadows, marked by lines
for schematic purposes—emerges, producing a more dramatic and complex
lighting effect.*

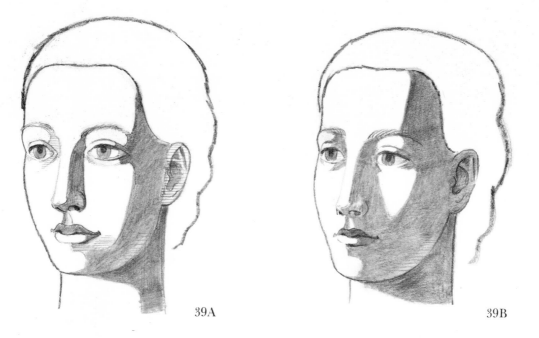

39A   39B

Figure 39A.   *Here the head is mostly in light, once again, with full light
falling on the forehead, cheeks, and frontal plane of the nose; the shadow
pattern is relatively narrow. 39B. As the light moves further to the side, more
of the head is in shadow and another characteristic pattern emerges.*

40A   40B

Figure 40A. *Here the narrow shadow pattern is seen from the other side; most of the head is in light. 40B. As the light rotates, most of the head falls into shadow or half shadow. Once again, these are characteristic patterns which should be committed to memory.*

Figure 41. *Light issuing from above is responsible for deep shadows in the eye socket and under the nose, lower lip, chin, and jaw. The somber lighting effect tends to overdramatize what should be a simple representation.*

Figure 42. *Although sculptures do not lose their plastic value (their three-dimensionality) when lit from both sides—because they are monochromatic—portraits appear flimsy when they are illuminated from more than one source.*

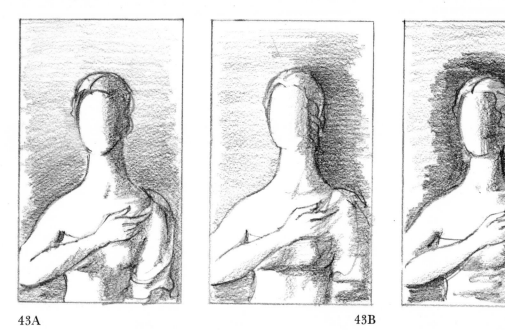

43A

43B

43C

Figure 43A. *The background is lighter at the top, where the light enters, and darker below, where the force of the light would diminish. 43B. The darkest area of the background meets the darkest part of the figure, where the model is in shade. 43C. The dark background gathers around the figure.*

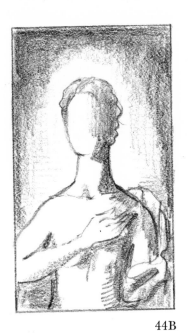

44A

44B

Figure 44A. *This is an unfortunate background lighting effect because of the strong contrast between the shadow side of the figure and the light area of the background. Moving from the darkened surface of the figure into the background, the eye finds no support and slips into the vacuum of light, which dominates. 44B. The darkness gathered around the edges of the picture creates an unpleasant halo of light around the figure.*

their sense of solidity and often compelling monumentality becomes apparent at once. By *classic*, I refer to the grandiose portraits of the Renaissance (Raphael, Titian, Tintoretto, etc.); for different esthetic tenets prevailed during the time of the Baroque—even though Baroque painters (Rembrandt, Hals, Rubens, etc.) would often hark back to the older system.

I mentioned that light generally entered the artist's studio from the side, as we realize from classic portraiture. Now you may say that such lighting was not favored by Rembrandt, a portraitist of the highest order. In his portraits, the area of shadow not only prevails over the light area, but the light quite often enters the scene from above. However, what worked well with Rembrandt did not do so well with some members of the 19th century academic school of portraitists who favored skylight illumination. For us, such lighting would be inappropriate (see Fig. 41) because it makes the model appear somber and overdramatizes what should be a simple representation of an individual.

Could we use a system of lighting that the Impressionists and post-Impressionists employed? Not very well. The problem is that the "system" was personalized, if we may say so, for each of these painters had a different mode of representation, in the absence of a generally prevailing esthetic ideology.

At the beginning of the 20th century, "double exposure" became fashionable; the idea was to light the model from opposite sides. As could have been expected, this "sophistication" proved to be fatuous. Portraits that receive their illumination from more than one source appear flimsy (Fig. 42). Still other spectacular means of lighting are absolutely devoid of any artistic merit. Hence it is best to limit ourselves to lighting that is seen in the charts of mnemonic light and shade patterns given here.

Lighting of backgrounds

It is self-evident that if the background is an interior of a room or a landscape, its lighting will most likely conform to the general lighting of the model. I say "most likely" because an interior *may* be composed of more than one compartment; hence, although the model (standing in front) may receive the light from the left side, the adjoining space (the room in the background, for instance) may be lighted from a different direction. In fact, such dual lighting may greatly enhance the total light and shade pattern of the picture.

However, even if a background represents a void—a plain, colored surface—the interplay of light and shade will produce various effects, all of which have one common task: to enhance the appearance of the portrait, as seen in Figs. 43 and 44. (In the illustrations, I have also noted unfavorable light and shade effects in the background, in relation to the figure.) Of course, the treatment of a background depends greatly on the general style of a painting. This treatment can be "conservative"—that is, avoiding strident or forced effects—or it may not conform to standard academic practices. The guiding principle in painting backgrounds should be simply this: *avoid* making the background too self-asserting—too active in terms of color, brush strokes, or texture which could weaken the effect of the figure. Also, very dark or very light backgrounds or strong colors are rarely the best choice, except when these areas are insignificant.

Plate 8. Julio De Diego. *Private collection. Another artist poses with a symbol of his calling, a canvas. The drama of the composition is emphasized by the unexpected placement of the sitter low in the picture. The long shadow in the background keeps him from "sliding out the bottom."*

45A   45B   45C

Figure 45A.   The head is placed centrally and the top of the headgear disappears beyond the frame, lending monumentality to the representation. Since the neck should not end at the bottom of the frame—an awkward termination—a few lines, suggesting a dress, improve the design greatly. 45B. The head tilts slightly to the right. This permits the head to be placed nearer the left edge without sliding out of the picture. 45C. The head is seen in profile, which also calls for wider space in the direction of the gaze; thus, the head is placed well away from the edge toward which the model is looking. 45D. Much of the background appears above the head and the shoulders take only a little space.

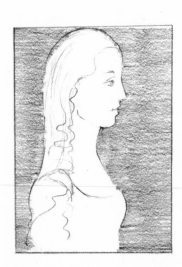

46A   46B   46C

Figure 46A.   The head is placed too close to the edge of the canvas on the side toward which the sitter is looking—thus forcing the viewer's eye out of the picture. 46B. The head is placed too high, almost touching the upper edge of the frame. 46C. The head is placed too low, giving too much prominence to the vacant background.

54

Chapter 8

Composing
the head
and shoulders

Composition refers to the arrangement of objects in space. In portraiture, composition is concerned with the placement of a head or figure on the canvas, hence the height and width of the canvas will be governed by this choice.

To begin with the smallest size, a 10″ x 12″ would be appropriate for a head, assuming that the head is just under life size. Generally, in portraiture, a size that is too small is rarely suitable, and too large a size should always be avoided. Besides, when working on a small scale, the painter is forced to treat a portrait miniaturistically, with a resulting tightness of execution. Over-large proportions of head or figure, on the other hand, belong to the realm of murals conceived on a heroic scale.

Favorable compositions

In Fig. 45, various placements of head and neck, and head and shoulders are seen. In Fig. 45A, the canvas would be 10″ x 12″; in Fig. 45B, the size would be 12″ x 14″; but variations such as 13″ x 15″, 14″ x 16″, and up to 14″ x 18″, or even occasionally 16″ x 20″, can also be used advantageously, depending on the nature of the subject. I would not choose larger dimensions for a head and shoulders because if too much space appears around the subject, the background tends to swallow it up.

When you paint more than head and shoul-

ders, the composition is ruled by the same principles that apply to smaller formats. Here are some suggestions for approximate sizes of canvas to be used for various occasions: half figure, 16″ x 22″ and up to 20″ x 26″; three-quarter view, 24″ x 30″ and up to 26″ x 36″. Should subsidiary elements enter a composition, different formats may be required.

Faulty compositions

There are certain irreversible rules when you compose a head or a figure on the designated space. For example, when the model faces a certain direction, the space in front of the head must be wider than that behind the model; otherwise it would appear that he (or she) is "walking out of the picture." If there is too much space above the head or figure, this space depresses the subject downward. When the outer contour of the head "hits" the frame, the beholder is apt to feel uncomfortable. But should a part of the head disappear behind the frame, the figure (or head) gains in monumentality.

Fig. 46 shows some of these typical errors in composition. Fig. 46A "walks out of the picture," literally forcing the viewer's gaze to the left hand side and focusing attention outside the frame. Fig. 46B "hits the frame." And Fig. 46C begins to slide downward out of the picture, leaving a weird, unexplained space above the head.

Chapter 9

Equipment for portrait painting

We may wonder whether portrait painting is a specialized branch of the artistic repertory. Indeed, it can be considered so and, as such, requires a particular choice of equipment.

Canvas for portraiture

Take the support, for example: unlike canvas which can be used for other purposes, the one suitable for portraiture should have a regular weave—not necessarily finely textured, but one that would not show knots, thicker or thinner fibers, or any irregularities. Whenever I have heedlessly failed to conform to this rule and have used one of my standard canvases (which I prepare myself), I have invariably found an insidious knot located precisely where it should not appear—on the nose, lips, and other such critical places.

I mentioned preparing a canvas myself; is there any justifiable objection to using a commercially prepared material? Not really—but I have a veritable phobia about it because of the mechanical appearance of the canvas sur-

Plate 9. Mrs. William Randolph Hearst, Jr. *The delicate, almost Botticelli-like appearance of the sitter called for a largely monochromatic treatment of the flesh and rather "precious" decor. The horizontal strokes of the background are an effective foil for the sinuous lines of the flowers and the figure.*

face. When prepared by the artist, the canvas has a different feel because, when the raw material is stretched, its woof and warp become ever so slightly disarranged; this irregularity gratifies the sensibilities of a trained eye. In Fig. 47, four principal qualities of canvas are represented.

The grain of the canvas in Fig. 47A is strong enough to hold the underpainting and overpainting without becoming slick because of the loss of tooth. In Fig. 47B, the tooth is so pronounced that it would require a number of paint layers to subdue it; hence such canvas is very difficult to manage. The canvas in Fig. 47C has a delicate grain suitable for very thin painting. Fig. 47D is suitable only for alla prima work because its tooth is too fine to serve for underpainting.

Preparing your own canvas

Although preparation of canvases has been described in some of my earlier books, here is the gist of the procedure, step-by-step, for those who *do* require this information.

(1) Stretch the raw fabric as tautly as possible on the stretchers.

(2) Start nailing into the wooden frame on one side of the canvas, then proceed with the corresponding side. Use upholstery tacks 3/8" long, and space them about 2" apart.

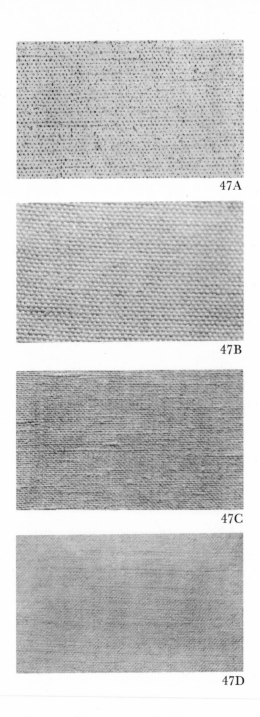

47A

47B

47C

47D

Figure 47A. *Commercially prepared, even grained canvas, good for general use. 47B. Single primed canvas, extra rough and hard to manage. 47C. Double primed, uneven, delicate grain, suitable for thin painting. 47D. Extra fine linen, single primed, suitable for alla prima work.*

(3) Apply moderate pull on the third side and nail it on. (Nailing can be done with a stapler more quickly and easily.)

(4) Finish with the fourth side, using maximum pull.

(5) Place one ounce of rabbit skin glue or carpenter glue in one pint of water. Soak it overnight in the water, then heat the water (in a double boiler) to dissolve the glue completely.

(6) Allow the glue to cool and to gel; this is the glue size that precedes the priming. Reduce the gel to mush with your spatula, and spread the glue size with the same instrument *very thinly*—first on the middle portion of the canvas—and spread to about 3″ away from its borders. This makes the canvas as taut as a drum. Proceed then to size the areas around the borders, again spreading the gel with a spatula. If you size a canvas that is not sufficiently taut, the underlying edge of the wooden stretcher bar will impress itself on the surface, and produce unsightly marks that are very difficult to correct. In such cases, a slight wetting of the reverse side of the canvas (the usual remedy to straighten out bulges caused through pressure of an object against the fabric) will generally prove ineffectual. Therefore, a more radical measure will have to be employed, such as pressing the slightly moistened area with a warm laundry iron. Of course, to do this, the canvas will have to be taken off the stretchers first.

(7) When the sized canvas has dried, its surface should be sandpapered, whereupon a second sizing should follow.

(8) Next comes priming with white lead; the best and cheapest material for this purpose is Dutch Boy white lead (in paste form, not paint) or a comparable product. The paste, as it comes from the can, is stiff; therefore it should be thinned with a little Copal Painting Medium. Apply the paste with your spatula *as thinly as possible*. In two or three days, give the canvas a second coat and allow it to dry for about a week before painting on it. This

48A   48B   48C

Figure 48A. *A bright bristle brush is particularly suitable for vigorous painting. 48B. The flat has longer bristles and will, therefore, leave a less pronounced mark on the paint texture. 48C. Soft hair blender.*

49A   49B   49C

Figure 49A. *The scriptliner is splendid for dashing delineations, but not for precise work. 49B, C. Standard round sables.*

all reads like a big order, but it really isn't. The procedures are quite simple and can be carried out even by the inexperienced.

If you buy a prepared canvas, be sure it is double primed so that the weave will not show deep interstices. This is important because most of your portraits will not need more than one underpainting—except for the face, which may need more corrective paint layers.

The category of canvas that has an almost silken texture will be used for alla prima painting (more about this later). This canvas should be single primed, for two layers of priming would take away all its tooth.

After reading this rather lengthy dissertation about your canvas, you may think that too much fuss is being made about it, and to what purpose? Now remember, if you will: our aim is to produce fine paintings—and no less— and our criteria of what is or is not fine comes to us directly from the great art of the past. Here and now, you have the choice either to become a disciple of the great old masters or to adopt the shoddy practice of the uninformed or lazy.

Brushes

Very few bristle brushes (Fig. 48) will be needed for portrait painting: two *flats* and two *brights*, No. 7 and 8 (or 6 and 7). For underpainting, the brights' shorter bristles allow for a more vigorous workout; and the longer flats are needed where the fluency of the brushstrokes counts. A larger brush, perhaps No. 10, can be added to these four brushes for painting larger surfaces, such as the background, dress, etc.

For painting small details, one round sable brush, No. 3 or 4 (watercolor size), will be required, and one No. 6 or 8, for dealing with larger objects (Fig. 49). One sable brush with extra long hair, the so-called scriptliner, will be most useful for producing "dashing" delineations: accents on the hair or dress, but by no means on the face, because this instrument is not suited for work where precision is important. To this array, add a soft-hair blender

—these are usually made of squirrel hair—about ¾″ to 1″ wide. And that ends our list of brushes.

Now you may ask why I have omitted the flat sable brushes, those capable (to use flowery language) of caressing the paint surface. These effete instruments, used for the softest touches, are really not needed when you dilute your paints with the Copal Painting Medium (described later in the text), because this medium will allow the most perfect and effortless blending of colors, even by means of the ordinary bristle brush. It is also true that strokes produced by the bristle brush have infinitely more character than those left by the soft sable brush. However, the decision whether or not to use such instruments must be left to the student's predilection.

Taking care of brushes

When you give your brushes good treatment, they will serve you well for a long time. And this good treatment is limited to washing the brushes thoroughly each time you use them. This is done with soap and water; special care should be taken to eliminate *every vestige of paint* which collects at the neck of the ferrule —that is where the decay of every brush starts. Here is an easy way to clean brushes. First, wipe them clean of all paint (newsprint serves best for this purpose). Then, submerge them in a glass containing foaming detergent; when you take the brushes out of this foaming bath, the residual paint will be well loosened and all of it will float away in a final soap and water treatment.

One thing should always be done to the round sable brushes: they should be left to dry in a perfect shape, which you can do best by pointing them between your lips. A sable brush that has lost its original shape becomes useless for painting features, although its fuzzy marks can register very well in accessories, dress, etc. As bristles can also become scraggy after much use and abuse, all you have to do to bring them back into their original shape is to wrap the wet bristles in a piece of news-

50A   50B   50C

Figure 50A. *Painting knife No. 1 is suitable for underpainting. 50B. No. 3 is a blender. 50C. Knife No. 2 is for finishing the portrait; the tapering, elastic blade operates on small areas with precision.*

print or paper towel, press them together tightly so they taper off toward the end, and allow them to dry before removing the wrapping.

Knives

First, it should be mentioned that a knife can be useful to the painter only when it possesses proper working quality. Second, it cannot be emphasized too strongly that once you develop skill in using this instrument, it will become just as important and indispensable to you as the brush.

I was just referring to "a knife," but one knife cannot combine all the qualities you will require in portrait painting. As a matter of fact, I have six knives in my own contingent which I call upon when I paint still lifes or landscapes; each one is shaped differently, but all have a *straight* blade. (The small trowel-shaped spatulas, so popular with the uninformed, are utterly inadequate.) My having such a large number as six points to my own predilection for this instrument; but in portrait painting, no matter how strong your penchant is for this instrument, all you will require are *three* painting knives.

These three knives—my own design, manufactured by Permanent Pigments of Cincinnati, Ohio—are seen in Fig. 50. Each knife has specific properties. Since the first (No. 1) serves for underpainting, it is stiffer than the other two because, in underpainting, paint of stiffer consistency is used, and you need greater effort to press the paint into the interstices of the fabric.

Knife No. 3, with the long and quite elastic blade, is a blender. It is capable of blending colors together and smoothing out brush strokes; these qualities make it a most impor-

tant tool for both underpainting and overpainting. When I discussed brushes a while ago, I mentioned that the one designated as No. 10 is suitable for painting the large surfaces that are generally found in backgrounds and clothing. Well, this is true; initially, a brush can, and perhaps will, be used exclusively for this purpose. But I always have the knife say the last word on backgrounds.

The No. 2 knife serves for finishing a painting; the elastic blade tapers to a narrow point, allowing it to operate on small areas with precision.

Painting with knives

All the knives mentioned are sensitive instruments; therefore they should be treated with great care. Never use them for scraping paint from the palette; you can do this with the sturdy spatula seen in Fig. 51. The painting knife should not be used when dry paint clings to it, because even the tiniest spot or impurity will mar the paint surface. When the edge of the knife becomes sharp from too much use, it should be dulled with a piece of carborundum paper; then the burr, which forms on both sides of the blade, should be removed. When the metal wears out and loses its straight edge, the knife is worthless.

If you ask me now how the knife should be used, at once I become conscious of the inadequacy of words. Only a few suggestions can be given here; the rest depends on practice and then more practice. All one can put in words is: operate only with the broadside of the blade; do not paint with the tip of the knife, which leaves an unpleasant texture in the paint body. The *narrower* the angle at which the blade is held toward the canvas, the more paint will be deposited. When you blend paint, hold the

Figure 51. *Scrape your palette with this spatula, never with the sensitive painting knives.*

61

blade in a position parallel to the canvas. The *wider* the angle, the more paint the blade will scrape off the canvas.

Painting mediums

Paint cannot be used very well in the consistency that comes from the tube—that is, not when you employ the technique that concerns us here. Therefore, depending on the occasion, your paint will have to be diluted, more or less, by a painting medium.

When I mention a diluent, the student will usually think of linseed oil, or turpentine, or a mixture of both. Because pigments are compounded with linseed oil to form "paint," linseed oil is often the first diluent that comes to mind. As for turpentine, what makes paints more liquid than this aromatic ambrosia? Suffice it to say that neither linseed oil nor turpentine will influence paint to behave as we expect it should.

To behave well—that is, to do our bidding —paint should have a resinous diluent, specifically, one compounded with a *hard* resin. Now, we have read in many old and more recent art manuals that ⅓ linseed oil, ⅓ turpentine, and ⅓ damar varnish, or any similar combination, will form a good resinous painting medium. Does it? The answer is emphatically no! All leading authorities in the field of paint technology—and I am thinking of scientific researchers and museum conservators— have unanimously rejected damar varnish as an additive to the painting medium. This soft resin (useful, however, as a varnish) will remain forever soluble to the action of a cleaning agent, no matter how mild, when the time arrives to cleanse a painting of the accumulated dirt that will sooner or later obscure its surface.

I mentioned that the paint "should behave in a manner expected of it." What exactly is this manner? A proper painting medium should promote fusability (the capacity of the paint to blend effortlessly), impart maximum depth to the color, improve drying properties, and allow a more efficient manipulation of paint.

As to the quality last mentioned, how can we achieve "efficient manipulation?" To understand this problem, one must know that tube paint has low viscosity. It is *short*—stiff, rather than fluid—because, in its manufacture, the paint receives an additive (aluminum stearate) to keep it in usable condition while it is stored in tubes. Tube paint, thus made, cannot be as efficiently manipulated as paint conditioned by the hard resin medium. Such paint will not act well in glazing and scumbling; it will not fuse easily; and it will not allow overpainting wet-on-wet—in short, it will not do our bidding.

However, a medium that possesses the requisite properties for all these manipulations, and available on the market for more than a quarter of a century, is Copal Painting Medium (Light and Heavy). It is manufactured from my formula by Permanent Pigments of Cincinnati, Ohio. Furthermore, when you use a medium compounded with a hard resin such as copal, both the toughness and non-porosity of the paint film will, in large measure, contribute to the painting's longevity.

Another ingredient of the same make, Copal Concentrate, is indispensable for making all paint manipulations more efficient. The concentrate is a thick, unctuous, semi-liquid substance that should be added, in small quantity, to *every color* before you start to paint. Add this medium in the following manner: as much of the concentrate as the tip of the palette knife holds should be thoroughly mixed with about 1″ of paint, as it comes from the tube. Too much concentrate will make the paint behave like enamel and it will become runny; paint conditioned in this manner is called *long*. Although extra long paint can be very valuable for manipulations of certain landscape and still life motifs, it has no place in portraiture.

Varnishes

We shall require three varnishes, each one serving a different purpose: retouching varnish, damar picture varnish, and copal varnish. (I am referring here to the varnishes formulated by me and manufactured by Permanent Pigments, for not all varnishes are of the same composition.) The first two are soft resin varnishes, used for varnishing after a painting has dried sufficiently. Copal (hard resin) varnish can also be used for varnishing pictures to great advantage, but (for us) its principal value is its use in alla prima painting, which I will discuss later.

What is the difference between the first two? Retouching varnish is the weaker one. It has a lesser concentration of resin and hence it should be used during the time when a painting cannot be considered thoroughly dry—that is, during a period of roughly one year. How soon can this retouching varnish be applied and why? As you will observe, your portrait will become flat and lusterless a few days after you finish it; the colors will sink in. To bring out the true appearance of these colors, you shall have to use retouching varnish, perhaps a week after you have finished the portrait. (The process will be described in a moment.)

Once this task is completed, can you sit back and relax? Not very well; in a few months, dull spots will reappear on the painting where the initial varnish film has deteriorated. On fresh paintings, the effectiveness of the retouching varnish is rather short; therefore, a second application may be needed. But, after a longer waiting period, we can consider the painting sufficiently dry to receive damar picture varnish. These will last on the painting—under favorable conditions—for a lifetime.

Now we shall discuss copal varnish, the most permanent of them all. Why don't we use it in the first place? Unless the painting is thoroughly dry (depending on the thickness of the paint film, this can happen in *one to three years*), such varnishing would be pointless. A *fresh* paint film, while it absorbs and releases oxygen in the process of drying, desiccates the varnish film on top of it. But when the time is propitious and the paint is really dry, copal varnish is a good choice. (Of course, for imprimaturas it is the only choice.)

Thus far, I have mentioned varnish only for revamping colors that have sunk in. But equally important is safeguarding the painted surface against atmospheric dirt and moisture. Dirt is one of the painting's greatest enemies: once it becomes incorporated into a paint film, its removal can become quite a problem. However, when the paint surface is protected by varnish, the discolored and dirty film can be easily removed. Even a film produced from our tough copal varnish can be dissolved without difficulty, if necessary.

Varnishing procedure

First, the painting must be clean. The superficial dust should be wiped off with a soft rag; then the more tenaciously clinging dirt can be eliminated by "massaging" the paint surface with your fingers. It is truly amazing how well your fingers will get the dirt out of your pictures!

When the surface is cleaned, place the painting on a flat surface in front of a window, and look at it from an angle that permits you to control the spreading, glossy film. If the painting is still fresh, use a soft brush and avoid undue pressure, because the varnish may easily soften a paint surface—especially the glazes, which are quite vulnerable. Take a little of the varnish on your brush and treat one small section of the surface at a time, perhaps 10″ square. On a firm and dry paint film, the varnish can be rubbed in with the side of your palm (using a circular motion); or a completely dry surface can be treated with a piece of cheesecloth moistened with the varnish. Spraying the varnish from a pressure can is totally inappropriate.

I have been discussing varnishing paintings done on canvas. Now, you may wonder about alla prima work (usually done on a panel). These paintings, if executed according to my directions, will never require varnishing—and the qualification "never" extends for an indefinite number of years. When I recently inspected a thirty year old painting, it appeared to me as it did when it was still wet.

Miscellaneous materials and equipment

For sketching before painting, *vine charcoal*

should be used in preference to any other material because its marks can be wiped off easily. Charcoal fixative will be needed to make the drawing on the canvas indelible.

When you draw, it is always advisable to do it first on thin paper (called transfer or tracing paper), and then trace it on to the canvas, using graphite coated paper for this purpose. You can make such paper simply by coating the back of thin paper with soft pencil strokes and blending them with a cleansing tissue. Carbon paper is entirely unsuitable because the traced lines will bleed, even through several paint layers. When you do a sketch on paper first, you assure the correct placement of a head or a figure on the assigned space. A drawing made on paper can be moved up, down, or sideways on the canvas before the transfer, so you can ascertain, in advance, which is the most favorable composition.

The need may arise to make a painting dry rapidly. You can achieve this by adding one drop of *cobalt dryer* to about a teaspoonful of the medium, and as much to about 1″ of paint as it comes from the tube.

Of course, you will also need an easel and a palette. A heavy and more elaborate easel is preferable to the light and flimsy kind which, as a rule, lacks the requisite stability.

The palette should be at least 10″ x 15″, or even larger. I use the top of a narrow chest of drawers for my palette; the chest contains all my painting materials, and is equipped with a wooden cover and rollers. It measures 15″ x 18″. The palette should be made of wood, rather than any other material, and its color should *not* be white! The reason for this rule (and it *should* be a rule) is simple: when we look at a white surface, our pupils contract; they expand when they meet a dark surface. Thus, when we use a white palette, our pupils are subjected to a tedious exercise. Besides, when color mixtures are produced on a white surface, they have different values from those found on the surface of a painting which is no longer white.

Color Plate 2 (Right). *Here the basic palette consists of three colors. Black, Venetian red, and white were used for the flesh tones in shade. White and Venetian red were used for the lights. Compare the over-all coloration of this picture with the effects of the four color palette in Color Plate 1.*

3A   3B   3F

3C   3G

3D   3H

3E   3I

Color Plate 3.

BLUES	*3A. Ultramarine blue and flake white.*
	3B. Prussian blue and flake white.
GREENS	*3C. Prussian blue, yellow ochre, and flake white.*
	3D. Prussian blue, cadmium yellow, and flake white.
	3E. Ivory black, yellow ochre, and flake white.
	3F. Ivory black, cadmium yellow, and flake white.
	3G. Viridian green, yellow ochre, and flake white.
	3H. Viridian green, cadmium yellow, and flake white.
BLUE-GREENS	*3I. Prussian blue, viridian green, yellow ochre, and flake white.*

66

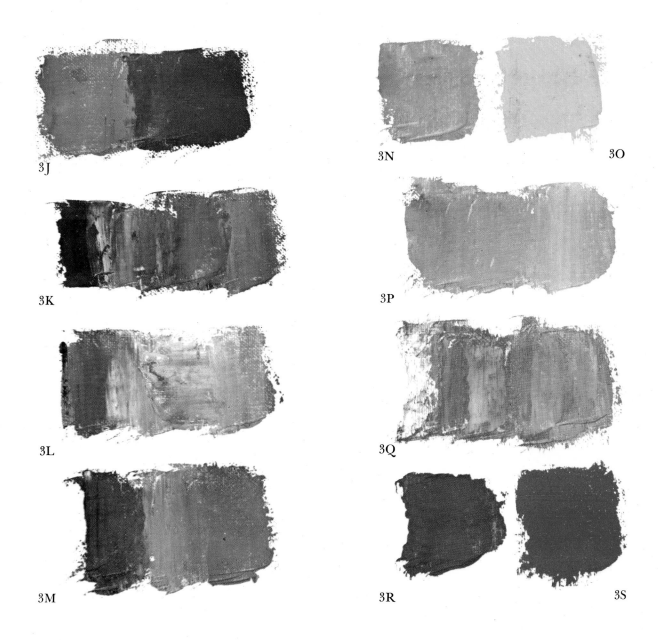

3J. *Ultramarine blue, viridian green, yellow ochre, and flake white.*

GRAYS

3K. *Prussian blue, burnt umber, and flake white.*
3L. *Viridian green, burnt umber, and flake white.*
3M. *Burnt siena, Prussian blue, and flake white.*

YELLOWS

3N. *Yellow ochre.*
3O. *Cadmium yellow.*

PINKS

3P. *Venetian red and flake white.*
3Q. *Cadmium red and flake white.*

REDS

3R. *Venetian red.*
3S. *Cadmium red.*

4A

4B

4C

Color Plate 4 (Left). *Various shades of toned ground for portrait painting. 4A. This tone is too light. 4B. This middle tone was mixed from burnt umber, Prussian blue, and flake white. 4C. Yellow ochre was added to produce a greenish tone.*

Color Plate 5 (Right). *This underpainting is done in neutral colors on a toned ground (see Color Plate 4): burnt umber, Prussian blue, and flake white on a toned ground of burnt umber and flake white. Characteristically, this underpainting is understated, consciously faded in appearance. The shadow side of the head is lighter than it will appear in the final painting, while the light side is somewhat darker than it will finally appear. The borders of shadow, hair, and eyebrows are blended and indefinite. Thus, the purpose of this underpainting is to establish the general distribution of light and shade, but to make no final commitment. All minute details are purposely omitted until the overpainting.*

6A

6B

6C

6D

6E

Color Plate 6. *Five examples of glazing and scumbling on various underpainting colors. 6A. Ground: yellow ochre and flake white. Glaze: burnt umber and ultramarine blue. 6B. Light gray ground: burnt umber, Prussian blue, and white. Flesh color glaze: burnt umber, Venetian red, yellow ochre, ultramarine blue, and flake white. 6C. Light green ground: Prussian blue, burnt umber, yellow ochre, and flake white. Glaze: burnt umber, Venetian red, yellow ochre, and flake white. 6D. Underpainting: burnt umber, Prussian blue, and flake white. Scumble: yellow ochre and flake white. 6E. Underpainting: burnt umber, Prussian blue, and flake white. Scumble: same colors as underpainting, but much lighter.*

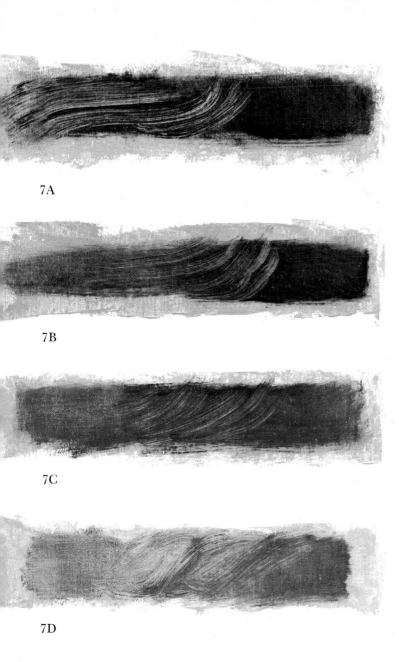

7A

7B

7C

7D

7E

7F

Color Plate 7. *Various methods of underpainting and glazing hair. 7A. Gray underpainting: burnt umber, Prussian blue, and flake white. Glaze: burnt umber and ultramarine blue. 7B. Underpainting: yellow ochre, burnt umber, and flake white. Glaze: burnt umber and yellow ochre. 7C. Light gray underpainting: Prussian blue, burnt umber, and flake white; or burnt umber, burnt siena, and flake white. Glaze: burnt siena. 7D. Underpainting: yellow ochre and flake white. Glaze: burnt siena. 7E. Underpainting: yellow ochre, burnt umber, and flake white. Glaze: burnt siena. 7F. Underpainting: burnt umber and flake white. Scumble: yellow ochre and flake white in the light areas; yellow ochre, ultramarine blue, burnt umber, and flake white in the shadow areas.*

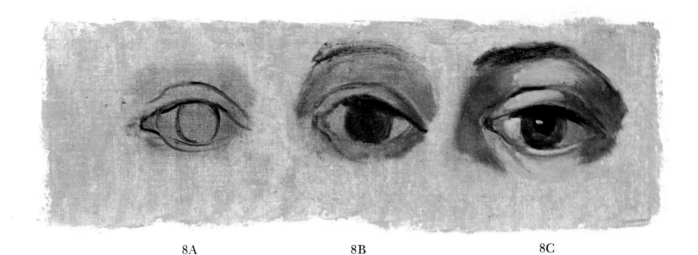

8A   8B   8C

Color Plate 8.   *Painting the eye, step by step. 8A. The entire surface is*
glazed with a middle tone. 8B. Major areas of light and shade, plus details,
are roughly indicated. 8C. Lightest and darkest accents, as well as the
highlight on the pupil, are added.

9A   9B   9C

Color Plate 9.   *Painting the nose. 9A. The entire shaded surface carries an*
unvarying tone. 9B. The lighter area is painted in. The raised surface
of the nostril—a bit lighter than the surrounding shadow—is wiped to
reveal the grisaille beneath or lightened with a touch of the brush. The
deeper shadow and middle tone are added. 9C. The entire shape is
modeled in detail. This view shows the complex shape of the nostrils.
Dark accents and highlights are added.

72

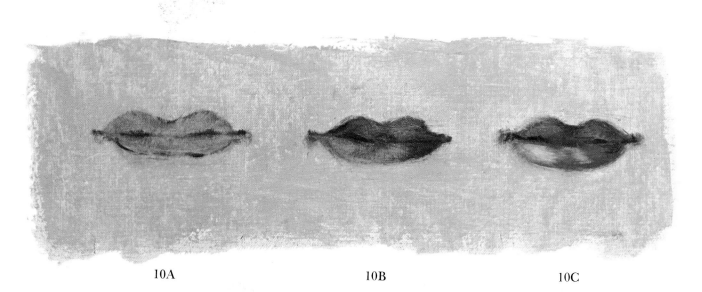

10A   10B   10C

Color Plate 10.   *Painting lips, step by step. 10A. In the first stage, the contours are roughly indicated in a flat middle tone, with a few accents added to define edges slightly. The forms remain evanescent. 10B. Darks and gradations are added. 10C. Highlights and deepest accents are applied. The edges remain soft throughout, so that the lips merge with the surrounding skin. Venetian red, burnt umber, and flake white were the only colors used.*

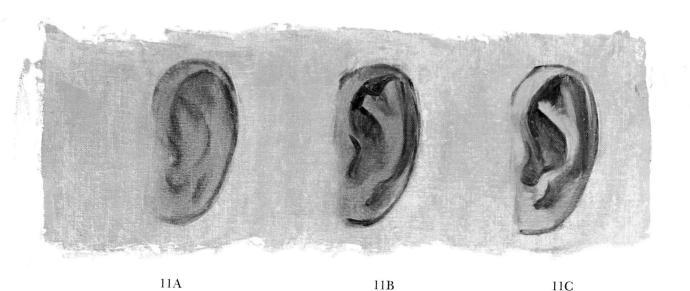

11A   11B   11C

Color Plate 11.   *Painting ears, step by step. 11A. A middle tone (burnt umber, Venetian red, yellow ochre, and flake white) is glazed over the drawing, which remains faintly visible. 11B. Into the wet glaze, shadows are painted. 11C. Highlights and dark accents are added and the entire surface is blended.*

Color Plate 12A.   *After one or more sittings with the model, the grisaille underpainting is completed. The sitter's features are established and the dress and turban are also underpainted. Characteristically, the over-all tonality is light and tentative at this stage.*

Color Plate 12B.   *The canvas is oiled with the medium—all or part of the surface, depending upon how much of the canvas we expect to cover at this sitting—and the shadow side is brushed in more decisively with the final colors. In the classic technique of the old masters, shadows are glowing, transparent glazes.*

Color Plate 12C. *Now the light passages are brushed in with ochre, some umber, and white. At this stage, neither the lights nor the shadows appear in full strength as yet.*

Color Plate 12D. *The lights and shadows are blended with the blending knife. This may also be done with a brush, the soft-hair blender or a flat sable. Now the painting appears slightly blurred and the drawing has been lost to some extent.*

Color Plate 12E. *Now the entire painting is gone over. Lights are made lighter; darks become darker; and the drawing becomes more precise. The reflection on the jaw is established by reducing the density of the shadow. This is done by wiping off the paint, revealing the light underpainting. The details of the eyes are painted —with crisp light and dark accents—and some red is subtly added to the lips.*

Color Plate 12F (Right). *The completed painting is an adaptation of Vermeer's* Head of a Girl with Blue Turban. *Here the turban, dress, and background have been given their final colors and the last corrective touches have been added. Notice the free brushwork in the collar and turban.*

76

Color Plate 13A. *This is the first phase of an alla prima portrait head done in one session. The imprimatura—over a ground of white acrylic gesso—is burnt umber, thinned with copal varnish. The lines of the preliminary charcoal drawing appear. The first rough indications of the shadows have been brushed in; they are glazes of burnt umber.*

Color Plate 13B. *In the second phase, the lights have been brushed in; the hair color has been suggested; and the first dark tones of the features begin to emerge. The light and shade are still understated.*

Color Plate 13C (Right). *In the final phase, the blending has been done with a bristle brush (the shadows as well as the lights) and the light and dark areas appear in full strength. The light and dark accents of the features have been added and the drawing has been strengthened. The background color has been added and the hair completed. The brownish color of the imprimatura prevails throughout and glazes predominate over opaque passages. The palette contained burnt umber, Venetian red, yellow ochre, ultramarine blue, and flake white for the flesh, and cadmium red for the background.*

79

Chapter 10

Colors and color mixing

For portraiture, very few colors will enter our palette. In my book on landscape painting, I have listed some two dozen colors; and this many would be recommended for still life paintings. But when it comes to flesh—of whatever complexion—only four colors will be needed (plus white). When we consider the background and some extravagance of costume, four or five additional colors should satisfy even a voracious appetite for a wide range of color.

As to parsimony in the choice of four colors, this may seem like a *non sequitur* because four colors can produce nearly "technicolor" effects, if such are desired; for it depends only on how they are intermixed. Later on, I shall explain how even two colors—for painting flesh—may suffice to achieve lively and wholly satisfactory effects.

Color Plate 14. *This alla prima head was done on a panel primed with acrylic gesso, then treated with an imprimatura of burnt siena, the presence of which is apparent throughout the panel. Characteristically, the lights are semi-opaque, while the shadows are transparent. Although knife work is unsuitable for large areas on a panel, small areas can be painted with the knife if this tool is used with discretion and restraint; notice the knife passages in the lighter areas of the headdress.*

Basic palette

At this point, you may be justly curious about which colors I refer to. Well, they are the most common variety: yellow ochre, Venetian red, burnt umber, ultramarine blue—and flake white, of course. Before we discuss the strategy of using these colors, allow me to assert—emphatically—that if you seek verisimilitude and a "classic" feeling, colors other than those recommended above should best be left alone.

Note the qualification that this is simply a *recommendation*; other painters, according to their own penchants, will call upon an entirely different list of colors. Your author's private color preferences extend in all possible directions, but these penchants can never serve the student well. Hence, in my approach to teaching, I have eradicated personal color idiosyncrasies and emphasized basic, universally useful colors. How often do I hear a student say: "But my teacher uses green earth for painting flesh." Well, if this color inspires *him*, his reasons are justified.

Incidentally, it is interesting to recount how prejudices, taboos, and sundry misinformation creep into some authors' writings, particularly those authors who—instead of arriving at facts empirically or consulting scientific papers on the technology of paint—rewrite, heedlessly, from ancient or altogether incompetent sources. Thus you hear false rumors about the deficiency of Prussian blue, umber, or some other excellent color, or you hear fairy tales about faults of copal resin, and so forth.

To return to the classic case of green earth, Cennino Cennini (14th century) states, in his venerable and renowned compendium, that he holds this color best for underpainting flesh. Cennini was right, but no later writers considered the fact that the ancient paint technologist was referring to *tempera*, not to oil colors! In an aquaeous solution, green earth is indeed valuable; but when compounded with oil, it turns into something resembling pea soup—with about as much tinting capacity. I may be digressing from our theme, but, in my opinion, a painter should gather as much information about his profession as he can.

Colors for flesh tones

Let us now discuss the rationale of our choice of colors for painting flesh. First, I mentioned burnt umber and ultramarine blue. What will their mixture yield? The answer is black and all shades of gray, when white is added. Could any other blue be used instead of ultramarine? Not for our purpose. Prussian and phthalo blue are far too aggressive; hence they will easily throw other colors out of balance. Also, Prussian blue tends to produce a strong green when mixed with ochre and this would aggravate the situation considerably by introducing a greenish quality in the flesh tones. The other blues available—cobalt and cerulean—would be equally inappropriate.

Our third color, Venetian red, has the right color value, but its tinting capacity is very strong; so a little of it will go a long way. However, in portrait painting, earth colors of identical value, but of far less tinting strength, can be used. These are known as terra rosa, terra di Pozzuoli, and light red—names used by different manufacturers.

When one of these reds is added to our gray (our mixture of umber, ultramarine, and white), how will it influence the mixture? It will make it warmer to a lesser or stronger degree, depending on the quantity of each color.

To follow out our reasoning, could we use cadmium red instead of an earth red? Well, if you like mauve and purple, you could; for cadmium, in the presence of ultramarine and white, would produce these obnoxious nuances. Although umber will improve the situation a little, the sickly color will prevail. Other existing red or brown-red colors cannot even be considered for painting flesh.

Next yellow ochre, our fourth and last color, enters the scene. What will ochre do to the existing ensemble? It will enliven it. With white alone, ochre will serve for the color of flesh as seen in full light. Here you may be troubled by the question: why not use cadmium yellow for this purpose? Do you know what this color would do to the umber-ultramarine mixture? It will turn it into grass green—a color too tough to be fought off easily. Of course, red could neutralize it, to some extent; but the resulting mess will surely defeat your purpose. As for Naples yellow, why should this cool yellow—wonderful for distant atmospheric effects in landscape painting—replace ochre? There is absolutely no reason for it; and there is no reason, at all, for using any of the other available yellows.

Let us now assume that we have mixed our four colors (and white, of course), and we find the mixture too gray. The remedy? Add ochre. Or if we find it too lively, umber will tone it down. Or perhaps we would like to make it warmer; red will do the job. If we want a cooler tone, we shall bring ultramarine into play; and if our mixture turns too green, its complementary color, red, will neutralize the unsatisfactory tonality. In short, you should *never* find yourself at an impasse when you use this set of colors.

Limited palettes

If we omit one or another of our standard set of colors, what tonalities can we expect?

If red is left out, the team of *ochre, ultramarine, umber,* and *white* will provide cool, green-grays. These hues will serve well when you want to paint flesh in a manner that is not naturalistic. That is, the realism of the representation will become subdued, not necessarily a disadvantage if this is the artistic effect you want to achieve.

The four colors mentioned above will act as follows. Ochre, ultramarine, and white will yield a dull green which is not too favorable a combination for our purposes; but umber will neutralize the mixture, thus making it agreeable to the eye. However, a different start would be more appropriate, namely to first mix umber, ochre, and white, then cool the mixture, gradually and judiciously, with ultramarine.

Therefore, it follows that how you begin mixing colors is important. Once a combination of colors has a considerable amount of white, it will become difficult to influence it, because white will tend to subdue any other color. But if umber and ochre are combined first, and ultramarine and white are added later, the mixture will become more easily controllable. In Color Plate 1, umber and ultramarine were used for flesh, with a small addition of ochre. White, ochre, and a little umber were used for the lights.

If we eliminate red from our team of colors, we reduce the lifelike appearance of the flesh, for it is the red that contributes chiefly to the naturalism of a portrait. But if we omit ultramarine, and work with just *umber, ochre,* and *Venetian red* (and white), a pink, ruddy complexion will appear, the kind we know from some portraits of the 18th century English school (particularly those of Raeburn and Lawrence). In painting children, you might very well employ this range of colors, which is capable of producing lively, delicate tonalities. However, for children, the use of umber should be limited, for it is a gloomy color.

If we now wish to simplify our palette even further and restrict it to three colors only, *Venetian red, ivory black,* and *white* will be a good choice (Color Plate 2). How will this combination operate? First, red and white will mix to a stronger or weaker pink, depending on the quality of red used. Black will simply gray the pink nuances, hence make the areas of shade cooler. For the parts of the face which are seen in full light, red and white will provide a bright, warm pink that will contrast

pleasantly with the gray-pink of the area in shadow.

But why use black, you may ask, when we have ultramarine in our original foursome: umber, ochre, Venetian red, and ultramarine. You are correct, of course; ultramarine and umber mix to a perfect black.

Colors for backgrounds and clothing

The colors I have mentioned thus far are ultramarine, ochre, Venetian red, umber, and black —five in all (besides white). All these were considered in connection with painting flesh.

Now we shall also be faced with painting the background, dress, and accessories—all of which will call for additional colors. In keeping with our expressed principle, *economy of means,* only five additional colors will be placed on our palette: Prussian blue, viridian green, cadmium yellow light, cadmium red, and burnt siena. Thus, our entire list will be composed of ten colors, plus white. (On the rarest occasion, alizarin crimson may be called for when you paint an extravagant dress or accessory.

Now let us consider what Prussian blue will do that cannot be accomplished by ultramarine. First, for mixtures of grays, this color is indispensable because none of our blues can match the range and beauty that Prussian blue, umber, and white can produce. Of course, ultramarine, umber, and white will also mix various grays, but their range will be much narrower and less attractive, because of ultramarine's purplish hue. (However, my aversion for purple nuances might again be due to a personal idiosyncrasy.) Furthermore, let us not denigrate the value of ultramarine in painting flesh obscured by shadow. Prussian blue will also be important for mixing greens (with ochre or cadmium yellow); for dull reddish blues (with Venetian red); and for darkest transparent greens, when mixed with burnt siena and glazed over yellow.

The next color I mentioned was viridian green. This will also combine well with umber and white, to create the kind of delicate grays we would use for backgrounds in portraits of children. (Why do I not mention a mixture

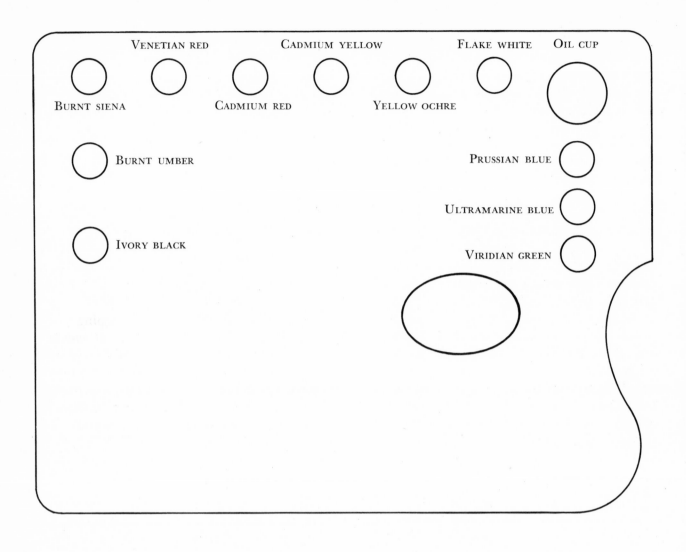

Figure 52. *Here is our entire portrait painting palette: ten colors, plus white. You may wish to add alizarin crimson to the red group.*

of black and white for grays? Simply because such grays are unattractive.) Mixed with cadmium yellow and Prussian blue, or with ultramarine and white, viridian will produce a variety of lively greens if we choose a landscape background. If we mix black, cadmium yellow, and white, dull greens will result. Of course, all these mixtures can be used for painting backgrounds, dress, etc., as required.

Cadmium red is our trump card, to be played out for decorative touches in dress, accessories, etc. Cadmium red, black, and white can be used occasionally for painting flesh. As for alizarin crimson, it can be used only for draperies, or to make cadmium red light turn dark through admixture.

Finally, flake white should be mentioned. It is—for our purposes—the best of all the whites offered on the market. It was also the only white oil color used by the old masters.

To recapitulate your entire range of colors, review many of the possible color combinations as seen in Color Plate 3. Our entire palette, arranged in proper sequence, is in Fig. 52.

Color characteristics

The student should be familiar with the following characteristics of colors:

(1) The more thoroughly two or more colors are compounded, the duller the mixture will appear. Hence for livelier color effects, brief mixing is essential.

(2) White will cut the intensity of all colors and reduce them to pastel hues. In some cases, white will alter the intrinsic character of a color: in its presence, red turns to pink; viridian green turns to bluish green; and alizarin crimson will entirely lose its original color (it will become an opaque mauve).

(3) Colors differ in their drying, tinting, and covering capacity. The quickest dryers are: umber, burnt siena, and Prussian blue. Even a small addition of umber will make every color mixture dry rapidly. Flake white, ultramarine blue, viridian green, ochre, and Venetian red all dry moderately well; cadmium yellow, cadmium red, ivory black, and alizarin crimson are slow dryers. However, different (often unhealthy) manufacturing methods may change the character of a slow drying color.

(4) Tinting capacity refers to the ability of a color to impart its own tint to other colors. The strongest colors in this respect are: Prussian blue, Venetian red, and cadmium yellow. (I have previously mentioned the milder but identical earth reds, preferable for use in portraiture: terra rosa, terra de Pozzuoli, and light red.) All other colors have good to moderate tinting strength.

(5) Covering capacity refers to the relative opacity of paints. Some colors are more, some are less opaque. To the less opaque category belong our blues. Viridian green and alizarin crimson are quite transparent; these are referred to as *glazing colors*. However, when sufficiently diluted by the painting medium, even an opaque color can be made transparent. Such is the case of burnt siena, a dull, opaque brown-red which, when diluted, becomes one of our most valuable glazing colors.

Chapter 11

Planning the portrait

At the outset of this treatise, I mentioned that portrait painting is a specialized branch of the art of painting, and as such, it is subject to particular disciplines.

Studio lighting

Take the artist's studio, for example. Unless suitable for painting portraits, it makes the work impossible, or at least very difficult. The studio window must admit daylight, but no *direct* sunlight. Even the least bit of sunlit surface in the room may, by reflecting light, falsify the appearance of the sitter's features. And a sunlit object outside the window, such as a tree or a building, will flood the studio with yellow glare. These are difficulties which may seriously handicap an inexperienced painter. However, a "hardbitten" practitioner will realize the limitations of such a situation and rely on his memory rather than on what he sees; in his mind, he will conjure up the ideal lighting condition.

And what are the ideal lighting conditions? The studio window should face the northern

---

Plate 10. Portrait of a Frame Maker (Alex Lazuk). *Private collection. Once again, the sitter's tools and working attire are eminently suitable accessories. The figure, receiving the full impact of the light, is set against a predominantly dark background, with one light area around his head.*

sky—with nothing nearby that could reflect yellow sunlight into the studio. If you are obliged to use artificial light, the model may receive a spotlight or a fluorescent light. This is a poor substitute for daylight, but experience will teach the painter how to cope with such a makeshift light arrangement.

How "truthful" can you be?

Many years ago, I painted a portrait of the leader of one of America's most aristocratic families. I omitted registering a purple discoloration which extended from the sitter's forehead to the root of his nose. When he viewed his likeness, my patron complained mournfully: "Where is the purple streak on my face?" Said I: "Sir, that isn't paintable." Retorted the old gentleman: "Young man, many a barrel of good whiskey went into the making of that purple—I want it in!"

This seems a logical time to observe that a portrait conception is really a compromise between what one *sees* and what one *knows*; for whatever one may see at a given moment, due to particular circumstances, must often be discounted. To mention a few common examples: a reddened nose due to a cold, a sunburn, or a blemish—painted as it appears in full light—will often suggest a shadow in a place where no shadows can be present, and thus confuse the light-shade relationship. Recalling a more

Figure 53. *Note the shadows around the eyes, nose, and mouth. Such shadows, which suggest deep wrinkles, should be minimized, rather than emphasized.*

Figure 54. *Note that I have purposely drawn the facial contour twice: once with a smoothly flowing line, and once with an irregular contour. The broken contour suggests age. Smoothly flowing lines are characteristic of young faces.*

drastic circumstance, how often have I seen a student paint a nude, sun-tanned model and conscientiously change from brown to white on those areas of the model's body that had been covered by a bathing suit and hence lacked a sun tan.

A most common mistake that I witness time and time again—even made by an advanced student of portraiture—is putting creases or wrinkles on a face where there are none. Usually, a shadow gathers in a facial hollow and proves deceptive (Fig. 53). It goes without saying that such a misapplied shadow will make a twenty year old person look twice as old.

When I talk about prematurely aging a face, remember that a successful portraitist is not necessarily a great painter, but one who makes a forty year old woman look like twenty. It is not uncommon at all to see a student use broken lines on a face of a very young person (as seen in Fig. 54), unaware that any break in a facial contour adds years to the subject's appearance. The contours of young faces always show smoothly flowing lines; thus, when we deviate from the model's appearance, it should be toward increased smoothness in order to emphasize youthfulness.

When I speak of emphasizing or de-emphasizing any characteristic of the model's face, do I mean that we deviate from the image we see before us? If so, is it right to do so? This reminds me of the client who, upon inspecting his portrait, inquired of the painter: "Is this my nose?" "Yes," was the reply. "And how about the eyes and the mouth—do they look that way?" "That is how I see them," said the painter. With obvious dismay the client turned to his portraitist and asked a very legitimate question: "Can't you cheat a little?" Now, it really is not a question of cheating or of being "honest," for the truthfulness of a painting has nothing to do with the painter's moral or ethical attitudes, but rather with his talent and his sense of those *esthetic* proprieties that are intertwined with his painting style and technique.

To discuss how far we can go today (or yesterday, or a hundred years ago) in "truthfully" depicting what we see, the answer is, not very far, indeed.

How far an artist steeped in late Gothic ideology could go, without infringing upon the esthetic probity of his art, is demonstrated in the work of Veit Stoss, the German sculptor (15th-16th century). His polychromed altar in the Cathedral of Cracow, Poland, is one of the great masterpieces of its kind. He faithfully depicted every deformity his models displayed: arthritic joints, varicose veins, and crippled limbs. But there is also an unearthly beauty in some of his figures—a beauty that would look sentimental and saccharine today. Had he the license to do such things? Yes, his time gave him this license—but I doubt that *we* could go so far! All this goes to show that depicting so-called reality is not as simple as it may appear.

Now, let us look at one of our own typical problems of "truthfulness." In *reality*, a shadow may register forcefully in certain areas of light; conversely, a light may be quite pronounced within the area of shade. Yet, when you paint these relationships, both the shadow on the light side and the strong light on the shadow side should be subdued; that is, they should be *subordinated* to the tone prevailing in the particular area.

Relationship of painter to sitter

Now, let us place ourselves in the studio so that the light enters from the painter's left side and the shadow of our right hand falls *away* from the surface we work on. Thus the sitter will receive light from his right side.

I referred to a sitter, implying that the model will be seated; you, of course, stand at your easel. This is preferable, for if you are seated, you become immobilized; besides you will tower above the model, an unfavorable artist-model relationship. The reason for this is simple: the lower a model is placed, the less of her (or his) neck becomes evident; the best angle from which the features should be viewed is from slightly *below* eye level. To repeat, the head of the sitter should therefore be a few

inches above that of the painter. Hence, we have to place the sitter's chair on a platform.

When only head and shoulders are painted, the model will be seated, of course, but this seat will not be seen in the picture. However, a half figure, when seated, will show the contraption upon which the sitter rests. Such a seating device should be minimized, if it cannot be concealed. Why should we be so bashful about a seat? Simply because modern chairs have no decorative allure, the modernism of yesterday is hideous, and the imitation of historic styles will impress us as fatuous. Now, I am not condemning all our chairs wholesale; I am merely stating that they do not lend themselves to pictorialization.

When you paint a three-quarter or full figure, the sitter may be in a seated or standing position. On such an occasion, you will, at times, find it more convenient to employ a substitute model (in the sitter's absence) so you will be able to paint the dress, and even the hands, in a more relaxed mood. With the old (and not so old) masters, this was standard practice.

Once the model is placed so that he receives the most advantageous lighting, how far away should we stand? Strangely, whenever a group of students gather around the model's stage, it is always at an impossible distance; even the one closest to it will stand as much as ten or twelve feet away! Now, if your eyesight is as keen as that of a hawk, you can maintain a distance of about six feet from the model when you paint the head and shoulders. A three-quarter length figure should be viewed from a distance of about nine feet, and you should stand still further away when the entire figure is being painted. This, however, applies to the whole figure only, not when you paint just the head.

Accessories and backgrounds

Now, we discuss an equivocal problem: how far can we go to "dress up" a portrait? First, literally, how should the model be *dressed?* Second, in what kind of setting?

As to dress, in our age of drastic changes in fashion each season, it would be foolhardy to follow any of the preposterous edicts of the fashion makers; hence the strictest simplicity should guide all our considerations.

Of course, there should be no hesitation in using decorative colors, as long as these do not *overwhelm* the sitter's image. Thus, we shall have to go easy on resplendent jewelry, flamboyant hairdos, opulent millinery, etc. Alas, the style of our time does not give us these decorative opportunities—Holbein, Velazquez, Gainsborough, and Goya did not have to suffer under such strictures!

In regard to female dress, common sense will dictate the proper choice. But what could be done when we face a Hart, Schaffner & Marx situation, aggravated by a starched, buttoned down shirt collar, and perhaps a bow tie? Whenever I have been confronted with such an emergency, my despair has been at its height. I wonder how a Frans Hals or a Rembrandt would extricate himself from such a predicament. Frankly, I have no idea how they could escape the discouraging sobriety of such a confrontation.

My own escape hatch, if I may call it thus, has usually been quite simple. If my model liked to steeplechase, I would paint him in his pink coat (which is really scarlet), or I would choose a polo shirt. When forced to cope with lapels, etc., I would treat the whole affair very casually and sketchily, veiling the sartorial trappings, so to speak, in a fog of ambiguity.

But, besides the attire, there are other pitfalls. In addition to the Hart, Schaffner & Marx debacle, should we put a book into the hand of our patron perhaps—or could we choose anything less corny? Worse still, to indicate his gentlemanly breeding and scholarly propensities, perhaps a whole library could be propped up in the background! And what frustration meets us when we consider a suitable prop or background for a member of the Polo Club!

In a condition of such frustration, what measures do we take? When we look back at precedents, seeking counsel—alas, precedents are of little help to us. Just call to mind the glorious landscape backgrounds or palace interiors of the Renaissance masters, the swirling draperies of the Baroque painters, even the elegance of the Neo-Classicists, or the sentimental backdrops of the 19th century Romantics. Could we follow in their footsteps? Hardly.

So, let us now carefully investigate how we can best extricate ourselves from our dilemma. Of course, there is always one equitable way out: a plain backdrop, involving nothing but color, some light and shade and paint texture. At times, we may use interiors with objects that suggest the sitter's calling—the tools, implements, or instruments of his profession. Such accessories will always be esthetically acceptable—that is, in good taste. We are intent on avoiding banalities and pointless imitations; thus, curtains, columns, and cozy or pompous interiors should be definitely ruled out. But the suggestion of a landscape motif or even a flower arrangement, if treated with tact and taste, would not necessarily stamp the work as trivial.

I wish there were rules covering all the imponderables of good taste in art—but, alas, there are none.

Plate 11. Portrait Study. *Private collection. A natural, informal pose—in clothes and hairdo that are classically simple—will hardly fail to be in good taste.*

90

Chapter 12

Underpainting

The preparation of canvas, as well as the ready-prepared commercial canvas, have both been thoroughly discussed. However, only white canvas was mentioned. Of course, one can start painting a portrait on the white priming, but, for this purpose, it is more propitious to work on a toned ground which carries a color, specifically a neutral grayish color.

Toned ground

This toned ground should be neither too light nor too dark; it should approximate the "middle tone" of the picture. The middle tone represents a color value which is darker than the light area of the flesh, but lighter than the darkest area of the flesh in shade.

The value of this toned ground is seen in Color Plate 4. As to the specific color, this choice is a matter of personal preference. The color of the toned ground can be neutral gray, greenish, brownish, bluish, or even pink-gray; more about this later.

Plate 12. The Artist's Wife. *Private collection. Memories of Rembrandt and the Tenebrists (Caravaggio et al.) must have been in my mind when I painted this. The figure emerges from shadow, which forms a dramatic pattern on her head and robe. Once again, the attire, hairdo, and architectural setting are simple, timeless.*

Whenever I make a statement that appears dogmatic, I must state the reason behind it. I consider this middle tone best for a toned ground because it ties together or *unifies* the tonality of a painting and provides a preliminary background for future paint applications. To demonstrate this point, consider a drawing of a head on colored paper, where the lights are registered in white chalk. At once, you will notice that the white marks establish the plasticity of form, while the color of the paper both unifies the tonality of the picture and establishes its background. (Such an effect appears in the painting by Goya in the final section.) Now call to mind a white canvas surface; on this surface, how well can you suggest a strong light by using light paint? You could not do it at all. In fact, the darker the color of the ground, the stronger will light effects appear on it.

A toned ground of the proper value allows glazing (transparencies) in the shadow parts and good registry of light. What is the particular virtue of transparent shadows? First, their texture is different from the opaque lights; hence, the textural contrast, in itself, offers an agreeable sensation to the eye. Secondly, shadows are intrinsically transparent: they are like veils that make the solid matter evanescent, just as light makes it concrete and palpable.

This does not mean, however, that transparency is the only way to treat a shadow. Certain schools, especially the Baroque painters known as Tenebrists (whose leader was Caravaggio, early in the 17th century), preferred opaque shadows. But the more translucent portraits of the Luminarists (late Baroque), show greater sensibility in treating textures.

To return to the color of the toned ground, I mentioned that its choice will depend on personal preference. Historically, the nature of the toned ground varied according to the country and prevailing traditions. Early Renaissance portraits—all done on wood panels—carried a white gesso ground. The toned ground appeared later in the 16th century; as a rule, it was a dark reddish color, like the ground Rembrandt worked on. Light toned grounds were common during the 18th century, although some painters (notably Goya, the greatest portraitist of his era) used a red ground approximating the color of Venetian red.

With the advent of the Impressionists (late 19th century), traditions disappeared. Generally, toned grounds were no longer used, although painters used nondescript turpentine washers to obliterate the white of the canvas priming and to serve as a kind of underpainting—though a useless one. Now, getting rid of the white color is a sound idea; for the white of the canvas (as well as a white palette) has a bad effect on the eyes. Experience shows that the reflective power of the white surface impedes establishing proper tonal relationships.

Various toned grounds

Let us now return to the specific colors of the toned canvas. I mentioned several, of which a neutral gray ground could be considered, perhaps, the most neutral. To be precise, a neutral gray can best be termed nondescript gray. This however, does not make it the most desirable color for our purpose; the most desirable color will obviously be the one that the individual artist likes best.

Gray, as we know, is mixed from Prussian blue, umber, and white—the fastest drying combination. Depending on the predominance of brown or blue, literally endless varieties of gray tonalities can be produced. Should we omit blue, umber mixed with white will yield what is commonly referred to as a fawn color. Such a toned ground is found in most of Gainsborough's paintings.

Another possibility is a greenish gray tone—very pleasant as an undertone for flesh tints. Umber, Prussian blue, ochre, and white are the best choices for this combination.

The last useful color for a toned ground could be a brownish pink. This warm color can be obtained from umber, Venetian red, and white.

How do you apply a toned ground to the white priming of a canvas? Before doing this, an important precondition is the tooth or texture of the primed canvas: remember that the additional layer of paint may deprive the canvas entirely of its tooth. Hence, smooth fabrics will not lend themselves to this operation, which must be carried out with *a knife and with rather stiff paint.*

The best material for this purpose is white lead paste, with the chosen color added. Should the paint be too stiff, a little Copal Painting Medium can be added. The thinnest possible film of colored priming should be applied, and all surplus paint scraped off. Under normal conditions, such a priming will be ready for painting in about a week. To accelerate its drying, a few drops of cobalt dryer can be mixed with a tablespoonful of paint.

Toned grounds aid rapid execution of portraits

To repeat, a toned ground facilitates rapid progress in painting a portrait—a work that can and should be done speedily.

That some reports (pretending to be authoritative) tell a different story, should not disturb us; for they issue from willful deceit or ignorance. To the first category belongs a report by the dealer, Vollard, who asserted that his famous portrait by Cézanne required 116 sittings. After careful study of the painting, I arrived at a more authentic figure of four sittings.

Life magazine once asserted that it took Matisse one hundred sittings to paint a portrait of his wife. Well, anyone taking even a cursory glance at the portrait (it carries no underpaintings, overpaints, or corrections), could see at once that a single short sitting was all that was needed to do this work.

Why are such tall stories disseminated by so-called experts and often by the painters themselves? The answer is simple: a great deal of labor is supposed to suggest the investment of a great deal of artistry and time, all of which should justify the amount of money spent on the painting. It is a well documented fact that even some of the greatest artists indulged in procrastination for no other reason than to impress their patron with the amount of care spent on behalf of the commission. A Gainsborough or a Goya could actually produce a finished portrait in half an hour, but how could they justify a high price for so little apparent effort?

There are, in the Prado Museum in Madrid, a number of studies of the members of the family of Carlos IV, whose group portrait hangs in the same room. The studies, made directly from the models, are painted on a red ground, in alla prima technique (with no elaborate underpainting), and the time required to paint each of them probably did not exceed thirty minutes. It is interesting to recount that the large group portrait—one of the most resplendent works of its kind—was painted from substitute models, using the original studies from nature for the likenesses of the participants.

Even painters who aimed at a perfect finish were capable of painting portraits in very little time. Writes Vasari: "The Sultan Muhammed asked Gentile Bellini to paint for him a self-portrait, which he did, with the aid of a mirror, in a few days." And in a report dated March 12, 1538, we read: "The Duchess (Christina of Milan) stood for Holbein from one o'clock until four. During that time he made a full length drawing together with a finished sketch in oil of her." We may also mention that while on his visit to Antwerp, Dürer, the meticulous

worker, painted the portrait of King Christian of Denmark, as the artist tells us in his diary, in one sitting.

All this goes to show that if the painter is skillful and uses a proper technique, a portrait can be painted speedily and well. I referred to the toned ground which is part and parcel of the proper technique, but I did not suggest that the artists mentioned used an underpainting for their portraits. Now, it must be understood that a toned ground is a kind of underpainting, precisely the one which corresponds to the imprimatura (a transparent veil of color) in alla prima painting done on a panel. However, it is far too extreme for me to suggest that a beginner should venture painting an alla prima portrait on a panel or on a canvas; for to do this right, you must not only be an assured draftsman, but a virtuoso who can make every brush stroke count.

Preliminary drawing

Assured draftsmanship is the *sine qua non* in portraiture! With this in mind, spare no effort to improve your facility in drawing.

It is a good plan to begin by making a sketch of the portrait on paper, rather than directly on the canvas. As every painter knows, it is easy to make a mistake in placing the subject properly on the assigned space; should you discover that an otherwise perfect drawing has been placed too high or too low, or too much to one side of the canvas, the entire effort would have to be deleted. But when the drawing is made on paper first, you can shift its position on top of the canvas—up and down and sideways—and the best placement can be easily found. Then the drawing can be transferred, using the graphite paper previously mentioned.

The question now arises, how far should you you go in finishing the drawing? Considering our procedure in painting, it would serve no purpose to carry out the preliminary drawing in detail, or especially to treat it in light and shade; for we are concerned with *outlines only*. However, the traced outlines, as they appear after the transfer, should be drawn over with charcoal to reinforce the weak marks left by the graphite transfer paper. Moreover, the charcoal drawing should be made indelible by spraying it with fixative.

General principles of underpainting

What is an underpainting? As the term indicates, it is one or more layers of paint that precede the overpainting or final layer of paint. This means that until the final stage of painting, we are still underpainting.

Now this underpainting can be methodical and serve a definite pre-calculated purpose, or it can be nothing but errors compounded. What, then, is an underpainting? We can say that it constitutes an understatement, in its literal meaning; that is, it must be considered a tentative attempt, a step toward the final rendition of the model's likeness. When we speak of an understatement, the implication is lack of emphasis. This lack of emphasis, this tentative groping, as it were, is seen in Color Plate 5.

What other purpose does the underpainting serve? We can speak precisely of two purposes: (1) to achieve a likeness by careful study of the sitter's features and the development of the light and shade pattern; (2) to create a color that could be exploited advantageously in subsequent stages through to the final painting. We may also add that the very existence of one or more underpaintings lends substance to the painting, and can enhance its textural appearance.

As a general principle, the color of the underpainting should *not* be identical with that of the overpainting, because the superimposition of identical colors is ineffectual. What results can we then expect when we paint *different* colors on top of one another? Providing that the underlying color asserts itself in some manner, interesting coloristic effects may be obtained. These effects can be brought about in more than one way. Obviously, the superimposed color may be transparent in various degrees, or the underlying color may simply remain exposed in some smaller or larger areas of the canvas, thus contrasting with the color or colors on top of it. We shall discuss these problems further in the next section.

Grisaille underpainting

The French word, *grisaille* (pronounced greez-eye), pertains to the use of gray colors in the underpainting; it is also called dead coloring or coloring in monotones. The method is an ancient one, dating back to the early Renaissance, or perhaps to a much earlier time. For us, the dead coloring for the areas of flesh is obligatory because nothing better has ever been devised to develop a portrait along the lines of classic technique.

To fully understand the value of the grisaille, let us consider for a moment what results we would get if—from the very start—we used full-blown colors for painting a portrait. (Here, I am not referring to alla prima technique, which is fully explained in a later section.) What would be our next step if we gave the flesh its florid polychromy at the very beginning? To finish the portrait to our liking, two or three overpaintings would be needed: at least that many corrective layers would be required to produce a likeness satisfactory to our patron. (His satisfaction, you must know, might differ from ours.) In this process, we would simply pile up two, three, or more identical polychromies—one on top of the other. The result: a gummed up performance —a pasty, pedestrian, unattractive affair.

But if we start with monotones (grisaille) of whatever coloration (cool gray, warm gray, dull green, or pink) and continue using this grisaille for as many sittings as are needed to establish a likeness, we will not require more than one final sitting to give our portrait definite color. Then, perhaps, we might need another sitting for final touches, especially those needed to improve the mouth and other troublesome details. How did Sargent put it? "A portrait is a picture of a person in which there is something wrong with the mouth."

So far, I have not sufficiently stressed the

aspects of the grisaille underpainting: its faded, bleached-out appearance; its characteristic understatement; and its lack of commitment to the true tones as we see them in the final painting. These understated tones (for we cannot speak of them as colors) are represented in Color Plate 5. In this plate, the area of light—as seen on the left side of the face—is *darker* than it eventually will appear. The area of shade is kept in a *lighter* tone than will be used in the final painting. Moreover, there are no definite borderlines of shadow, hair, or eyebrows; in short, all the contours are softly blended and minute details are absent.

Grisaille procedure

Now to the salient points of the grisaille procedure.

(1) The paint used for this purpose should be as stiff as possible; any undue dilution by the painting medium must be avoided. Of course, if the paint is too stiff to be easily moved by the brush, some medium should be added.

(2) The toned ground should *not* be moistened by the medium (our usual procedure before starting to paint). Also, there is no need for the Copal Concentrate, which is always added to our colors in the *final* stage of painting. (In the underpainting, we do not aim at fluency of brushstrokes or improved fusability of colors.)

(3) *Always start with the shadow area of the flesh*, one of the irreversible rules of oil painting: the darks first, next the lights.

(4) Use the same gray colors for flesh, eyes, and mouth, but not for hair. The technique which we are employing calls for the use of true glazes in painting hair. The reason for this preference is simple: our aim is to create as much textural variety as the occasion allows, and glazes and impasti (thick passages) are responsible for textural effects.

(5) Start painting with two bristle brushes, one for the lights, the second for the darks (brights No. 7 or 8). Paint freely, without too much blending, which will be accomplished later with the painting knife called the blender.

(6) By holding the knife almost parallel to the painting surface, and by moving it swiftly first in one direction, then in another, perfect blending of paint can be produced—if the canvas has sufficient tooth (texture) to take in enough paint material to fill the interstices of the fabric. Whether or not this clogging of the interstices has been accomplished becomes apparent when you hold the canvas toward the light. Light falling at an angle onto the surface—so-called raking light—will clearly show the depth of the fabric's interstices.

(7) At this stage, the design of the face has become fairly obliterated. To restore facial patterns, use one of the small round sable brushes and some umber diluted by the medium; reestablish the lost drawing by marking it faintly in the relevant places.

It should be understood that the underpainting must be *perfectly dry* before you paint on it. Further, if the first underpainting (grisaille) proves unsatisfactory, a second, third, or more of the same can follow because when you paint in grays, you cannot "gum up the works."

Until the last phase of painting, the background remains unchanged; its color will be the same as the original toned ground. However, should you wish to blend the outer contours of the figure with the background—a procedure which is often essential—paint a narrow strip of the background around the figure, then blend it with the grisaille, first using the brush, next the knife.

Blending

Why do I stress blending and why should the knife be the last tool to leave its effects on the canvas? The answer is: once the contours are blended in the underpainting, the problem of blending them in the final painting becomes greatly simplified. And should you wish to define the contours strongly, here or there, you can do it at any time.

Furthermore, filling in the fabric's interstices in the underpainting is of paramount importance. This job is not for the brush, which deposits the paint material on the ridges as well as in the declivities of the weave; hence, the brush increases rather than diminishes the roughness of the fabric. If we continue to work with the brush (always on top of a dry surface) and thus pile up high impasti, a rich web of paint will result. While this texture has its value in certain techniques and fulfills a legitimate esthetic purpose, it is not suitable for classic portraiture. Here the smoothness of the underpainting is essential, for we are concerned with the texture of flesh as conceived by masters who worked in the classic tradition.

Since I have referred to the classic tradition on many occasions, it behooves me to repeat: the classism I refer to (there are many divergent classic traditions) is most clearly exemplified in the work of Gainsborough (18th century), Goya (18th-19th century), and later Degas (mid-19th to early 20th century).

Glazing

Paint transparency has been mentioned repeatedly, and I have also stated that transparency can be produced by simply diluting the colors with painting medium; nothing could be simpler. However, the conditions under which transparencies can be properly used are not so simple: a transparent color (we call it a *glaze*) can be activated only when certain preparatory measures are taken—specifically, when a proper underpainting is first provided.

Glazing is an ancient technique. It was known early in the history of painting, and was specially favored during the Renaissance, when painting was not a matter of improvisation, but was planned methodically.

Let us now investigate the method. *A glaze must always be darker than the underlying color.* The lighter the underpainting color, the more active the glaze will be. Although glazes can be applied to a white surface, too, such a surface will not impart its color to the glaze. This points to the importance of the color underlying a glaze, which frequently influences the glaze to make it lose its coloristic identity.

Glazes must be executed on a perfectly dry surface, with the copal medium previously described. Because the color used for glazing is thin, a viscous medium (called Copal Painting Medium Heavy) is more appropriate for this purpose.

As I previously stated, any color (except white), will be suitable for glazing, when sufficiently diluted with the medium, for all practical purposes, we shall be concerned with only four colors: umber, ultramarine, burnt siena, and viridian green.

I should mention that we shall distinguish between the definition of *glaze* and *true glaze*. *Glaze* refers to any transparent color, even one containing white, in which case the color will really be semi-transparent. The second term, true glaze, represents a pure color *without* the admixture of white. White, even in small quantity, will always reduce the transparency of a glaze.

In portraiture, we can use transparent color applications first, when we paint the hair of the model and flesh as it appears in shade (lights are opaque); secondly, in connection with painting dress, accessories, and background.

Scumbling

Scumbling is just the reverse of glazing. Here, a light color—one that as a rule contains white—is applied to a darker surface. And this application is usually done while you paint into a wet surface (not as in glazing, where the surface must be dry). In short, whenever you paint a lighter color onto a darker surface, and allow the darker surface to remain in evidence, you *scumble*. This implies that the lighter paint is not entirely opaque, because, if it were, it would conceal the presence of the underlying darker surface.

Whereas appropriate surfaces for glazing must be prepared in advance, scumbling can be done at any time; a light surface can be darkened for scumbling at will, simply by using a glaze or a solid paint layer. Also, there is no need to wait until this darker paint dries. Actually, scumbles are more effective when done into a wet glaze or into a solid, wet paint layer.

But the wetness must have a special quality: namely, *high viscosity*; otherwise, carrying out the scumbles would be quite difficult. Therefore, all colors should be conditioned by Copal Concentrate. An important thing to remember: unless done on a dry underpainting (dry, but always moistened by the medium), scumbles are executed with the painting knife, not with the brush. The reason for this rule is simple: the bristles would dig too deeply into the wet layer of paint, or churn up the glaze. However, the knife deposits the color without unduly disturbing the underlying paint strata or glaze. In some exceptional cases, a soft flat sable brush—moving liquid paint—could be used to produce scumble effects on an especially viscous surface.

Chapter 13

Painting
details
of the head

It may sound odd when I advise the student to begin by practicing painting the features out of context, as it were, and then to put them in the usual order on the face. But experience has taught me that better progress can be achieved by giving one's attention to details first; it is, in fact, like learning the meaning of words before putting them together to make sentences.

Hair

To start at the top (literally), how do you paint hair? I alluded to this problem briefly in connection with glazing and scumbling, and the point bears repeating: in order to differentiate between the textures of hair and flesh, observe the dissimilarity of their surface qualities and treat them first in true glazes. (As we remember, true glazes are those that contain no white; they are pure color only.) As we know, the color of the glazes largely depends on the color of the underpainting which, in

Plate 13. Emperor Jones. *M. H. De Young Memorial Museum, San Francisco, California. The cadmium red tunic was underpainted in a dull blue-green (Prussian blue, ochre, and white). A yellow-green underpainting (Prussian blue, cadmium yellow, and white) appears wherever the effect of gold was sought. The background began as pink and ended, finally, as dull green.*

this case, will be the *color representing the highlights on the hair.* This procedure is demonstrated in Color Plate 7. On the left hand side of each example, the underpainting appears in its original color, which comes through the glaze as highlights.

In Color Plate 7A, the underpainting was a light bluish color: Prussian blue, umber, and white; the glaze was ultramarine and umber, giving a dense black. Here the black hair appears as if it has bluish highlights. These highlights were obtained by wiping the glaze, in appropriate places, with a piece of cheesecloth (or a stiff brush), *thus allowing the underlying color to serve as the final color.* In the actual painting of a portrait, the marks of the cheesecloth would be augmented by those produced with a scriptliner or a round sable brush.

In Color Plate 7B, we assume that the hair color is dark brown, in which case the highlights may appear to be a yellowish color. Hence, the underpainting will be prepared from ochre and white. (To remind the reader, white should be added to every color in an underpainting.) When white is mixed with a light color such as ochre or siena, a very light tone will result. Now, when you paint dark hair (of whatever color), a glaze applied on top of such a light tone may be too luminous; as we know, the lighter the underpainting, the more luminous the glaze. Hence we may apply the light underpainting *only in the area of the highlights*. In the area of shade, the underpainting may be darker: ochre, umber, and white. Such two tone underpainting would correspond to the underpainting in grisaille which carries a lighter and a darker tone blended together.

In Color Plates 7C, 7D, and 7E, things become more lively, for here we paint red hair, which calls for considerable ingenuity. Depending on the specific hue of the hair—ranging from carrot color to what is generally referred to as auburn, a rich brown-red—our underpainting may carry the following colors. Color Plate 7C is underpainted in light gray: Prussian blue, umber, and white; or umber, burnt siena, and white. Color Plate 7D is underpainted in ochre and white; in some cases the hue of ochre could be heightened by a small addition of cadmium yellow. Color Plate 7E is underpainted in ochre, umber, and white. All are glazed in burnt siena. Remember: all these underpaintings will represent the color of the *highlights* in the hair, conditioned in some measure by the glaze of *burnt siena*.

It may surprise you that burnt siena is the only color that we shall use for painting whatever shade of red hair. The transparent burnt siena (that is, diluted by the medium), together with the color of the underpainting, will be our middle tone. As always, the highlights will be derived by wiping the color away from the underpainting. And how about the deepest shadows? Black mixed with burnt siena will provide the right effect. I suggest that you familiarize yourself with the effects of various underpaintings and glazes; these experimental efforts should be carried out as an independent exercise.

Color Plate 7F does not involve as clear-cut procedures as the foregoing. Because blond hair may range from the lightest to blond-brown, different technical treatments will be called for. As we know, we cannot produce a glaze with a very light color because the glaze then requires the admixture of white. It is true that ochre (the lightest color on our palette) could be glazed on a white underpainting, but such a glaze would be quite unattractive: it would merely stain the white underpainting

with a yellowish color. How can we deal with such a contingency? Opaque painting is the answer, with a scumble of ochre and white in the light areas; and ochre, some umber, and perhaps a dash of ultramarine in the shadow parts—all over an underpainting of umber and white.

Eyes

Perhaps in no other subject are beginners' errors so compounded as in painting eyes.

Let us start with the eyebrows: because hard, well-defined eyebrows are ugly, they should be lightly brushed on. We shall indicate the brows' presence ever so slightly in the underpainting; but they will be the last to be finished—after all of the eye and the surrounding area are done. Their contours, especially where they terminate at the temple, should be blended to avoid that "penciled" look.

As for the eye itself, the cardinal mistake of the student is to paint the white of the eye, the iris, and the pupil as *separate* units. In Color Plate 8A, the first step of the correct procedure is seen. Here the entire surface of the eye and eyelids is covered thinly by a *middle tone*, that is, with the color of flesh which is neither in full light nor in full shade. In this example, the colors used are standard (but kept on the cool side): umber, Venetian red, ochre, ultramarine, and white. They are thin enough to be considered a glaze and they are used to unify the tonality of the object.

This unity is important because nothing looks more awkward than having the eye "fall apart" into its diverse components. The white of the eye, especially when it is not painted into an underlying (darker) wet color, will appear hard, like porcelain. The iris and the pupil, too, may show a certain disconnection. Of course, blending all the details would eliminate the hard contours and promote unity, but blending colors will be greatly facilitated when they are painted into the wet glaze (Color Plate 8B). Moreover, the glaze will impart some of its own color to the superimposed color, which is one of the chief factors in achieving over-all unity.

In Color Plate 8C, a highlight has been added in the pupil. Now, use of this highlight is of doubtful advantage. It adds life to the eye, no doubt; but it is questionable whether the life-like or (more accurately) the stark naturalistic effect is desirable in portraiture conceived in our time. Here again we shall have to fall back on our guiding principle: discretion in handling everything that may become too obvious.

Also, in the same example, the final touches of light and the deepest shadows are painted into the still wet middle tone. When we examine this sketch, it becomes clear at once how unwise it would be to paint the light effect separately on the small surface of the upper eyelid. The light color (ochre and white) has enough strength to register its value even when it is painted into the wet middle tone. Now, as all painting is done into this wet middle tone, a perfect fusion of colors is attained with ease and elegance.

About painting eyes, two important rules should be noted (Fig. 55). The upper border of the pupils should always be covered by the upper eyelashes. That is, the iris should not be visible above the pupil; otherwise, the eye will take on a fixed glare. Such a piercing look in the model's eye, emphasized by the highlight in the pupil, can become quite disconcerting. The configuration of the eyelashes is also very important. They do not form an unvarying frame along the border of the upper eyelid: their appearance changes as the eye turns, and they are longer in the middle than at the sides.

Lastly, the surface of the eyeball is not flat, but spherical; hence the light and shade effects on it will conform with its shape. Although all these effects are plainly visible on the model, unless you are conversant with these fundamentals, you will not easily discover them. Here, as always, a knowledge of structure is necessary before you begin painting.

Nose

All the facts about the construction of the nose were discussed in Chapter 3. Painting the

55A

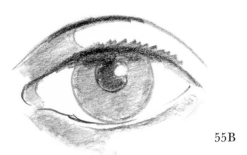

55B

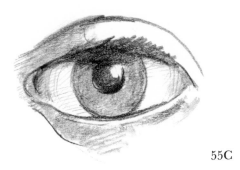

55C

Figure 55A. *When too much of the iris is visible, the pupil takes on a piercing, disturbing look.*
55B. The eyelids vary in length—longer in the middle than at the sides—and their appearance changes as the eye turns. 55C. The light and shade effects on the eyeball and lids conform to the spherical shape of the surface. Note the cast shadow of the upper lid.

nostrils, however, will pose certain problems with which you should familiarize yourself. These are exemplified in Color Plate 9.

In Color Plate 9A, the light enters from the left side. As usual, the nostril on the side of the shade will be a little lighter than the rest of the surface on that side of the face. But, we shall not take this into consideration at first; so the entire surface will be painted the color of the shade. It makes no sense to save this insignificant area for a lighter definition. This lighter tone is easy enough to produce later, in one of two ways: wiping the shadow off at the spot with one's finger or a piece of cheesecloth would uncover the light grisaille underneath; or a flick of your brush, carrying lighter paint, can do it (Color Plate 9B). Now there remains the external opening of the nostril, which is a complex configuration (Color Plate 9C) —not a round hole drilled into the root of the nose.

An important final note about the nostril color: it should not suggest black. Hence, mixtures of umber and ultramarine (which one would be tempted to use for the darkest definitions) must be ruled out because a cold, dark color in this particular place would rob this feature of its life; the nose would look cadaverous. Why this should be so I do not know, but the fact is that in portraits that are most lifelike (recall Rubens, for example), the nostrils and some areas around the ears are often painted a brilliant red. Now we shall not go that far, but a warm color—just plain burnt umber, with or without a trace of Venetian red—will have to be our choice.

Mouth

I have mentioned the difficulty the portraitist often encounters when he paints the model's mouth. This problem comes from the mouth's mobility, hence, the instantaneous change of expression that comes about with its slightest movement. The experienced artist, for example, knows that it is not the eyes, but the mouth which gives the face a gay or a sad expression.

How does a mournful countenance appear? Simply by a downward turn of the mouth's

corners. But should such a turn actually be seen on the model's face, never, never let a pout show on your canvas or you will fail inexorably in your effort to please the patron. Always keep the corners of the mouth upturned just a little; this advice, corny as it sounds, may save the day for you.

As I have mentioned, undue animation—flashing teeth, broad smiles, etc.—must also be avoided. Good taste legislates this, but it does not rule out the expression of slight animation.

Another difficulty is how to make the mouth part of the face, not a foreign element added onto it; this problem is analogous to the pasted-on look of eyebrows, previously discussed. Therefore, avoid hard contours of the lips and try to achieve soft transitions from one plane to another, corresponding to the characteristics of the shapes. This treatment is seen in Color Plate 10 in which the contours are first evanescent and later more strongly accentuated; a *uniform* blending of the lips' outline would not be consistent with their configuration.

As for colors, here you should be particularly restrained, and keep tubes of cadmium red and alizarin crimson tightly closed, unless you plan to compete with lipstick ads. And since I have mentioned lipstick, remember to have your model immediately remove its marks from her lips, so that you may realize their true shape. Then you will select your colors, which should have the *least* flamboyant nature: Venetian red for the middle tone; the same color, with white, for the lights; and mixed with umber for the darks.

Ears

The intricacy of the ears' convolutions was dealt with in Chapter 3. However, they are simple to paint once we can rely on a proper drawing. Color Plate 11 illustrates the entire procedure and, at the same time, shows the principles of the painting techniques with which we are concerned.

In Color Plate 11A, the drawing appears faintly visible under the obscuring glaze: a middle tone mixed from umber, Venetian red, ochre, and white. In Color Plate 11B, only the shadows were painted, as usual, into the wet glaze. Finally, in Color Plate 11C, the entire surface was carefully modeled and blended with a soft bristle brush. This can be done successfully only when there is enough viscosity in the paint. If there is not, a soft-hair blender should be used.

106

Chapter 14

Painting
a head
in colors

After all these exacting preliminaries, we shall now attempt to paint a portrait. Although I may be accused of prolixity, I cannot refrain from restating the problems of color in portraiture.

Tonality vs. polychromy

In painting, the choice of color is dictated by taste—that sea of uncertainty! Hence, in choosing a color scheme for a portrait, a clarification of specific issues seems to be in order.

To illuminate the subject, allow me to quote from one of my essays: "To pinpoint the problem: color and form are engaged in a perpetual warfare, nip and tuck—here one wins, there it loses." In short, we shall have to accept the rule that the more monochromatic the form, the more monumental and unified its effect.

There can be no doubt about it: in our time, we have no license to paint rosy cheeks and sparkling lips à la Sir Thomas Lawrence, Raeburn, etc.; or to employ polychromy à la Holbein; or to exuberate in the flamboyance of a Renaissance master. Why? Because such things have moved into the precincts of calendar art and magazine covers; this sort of pictorialization fails as art because of the onus of the vulgar and commonplace that has been attached to it. Hence, in choosing colors, discretion will be our guiding principle.

What is a discreet color as opposed to polychromy? The first is a broken color, specifically broken by white which reduces its activity and produces gradations of color, rather than color contrasts. Polychromy, on the other hand, aims at contrasts, playing one strong hue against another.

Summary of painting procedure

Let us turn to the procedure of painting a head in color, step by step, as illustrated in Color Plate 12. Before dealing with such specific problems as color, backgrounds, etc., let me summarize the sequence briefly.

Step 1 (*Color Plate* 12*A*): Now we have had one sitting with our model (or two or three sittings) and we have finished our grisaille, or as many graisailles as were needed to establish the sitter's features satisfactorily. At this stage, the dress and the turban have also been underpainted.

Step 2 (*Color Plate* 12*B*): How shall we continue and prepare for Step 2? We can do one of two things: we can brush the medium over the entire canvas, background and all (after

Plate 14.   William Gerstle. *San Francisco Museum of Art. An industrialist and a great art patron, the sitter was also an amateur artist—a fact which determined the pose, dress, and accessories.*

it has dried, of course), if we expect to finish the work in one day. Or if we plan to concentrate on the face during this sitting, we apply medium on this part only.

To repeat: *oiling between dry underpaintings is not necessary* because, at this stage, we are not concerned with the fluency of brush strokes or the ease with which blending of colors can be accomplished. But when we apply colors, both these qualities—the fluency of brushstrokes and the ease of blending—are important and oiling becomes necessary. But remember, when a portion of the canvas remains oiled, but not painted, wipe off the medium with a turpentine-moistened rag; we must not allow the medium to dry because this will make the surface slick. To sum up the preceding: before starting to paint with final colors, *oil the surface.*

Another alternative is to cover the entire grisaille with a glaze of our standard mixture: umber, Venetian red, ochre, ultramarine, and white, thinned with the medium to a rather liquid consistency; then start painting into the wet glaze. However, this procedure should not be attempted by the inexperienced.

As usual, we start painting the shadow side first, and, at the same time, we try to revamp and refine the drawing.

Step 3 (Color Plate 12C): Here the lights are brushed in with ochre, some umber, and white; but these colors, as well as the shadows, do not appear in full strength as yet.

Step 4 (Color Plate 12D): Blending is carried out with our blending knife, called the blender. Because there is still some tooth left on the canvas, the blending proceeds effortlessly. Blending with the knife is really a simple operation—though perhaps not for the novice. To make it easier, one may at first use the soft-hair blender or, still better, a flat sable brush.

Step 5 (Color Plate 12E): After the blending, the painting appears blurred, and the drawing has also been lost to some extent. So the entire initial painting is gone over: the lights are made lighter, the shadows darker, the drawing more precise, and the reflection on the jaw

established. Also the eyes, with all their details, are painted. Then some red is applied to the lips.

Step 6 (Color Plate 12F): The turban, dress, and background are given their final colors, and a few more corrective touches are added. The demonstration painting is an adaptation of a great portrait by Vermeer, *Head of a Girl With Blue Turban.*

A note on reflections

Another detail for consideration is the reflection at the edge of the jaw. Reflections are light effects in the area of the shade, cast by a light object—here by the model's white collar. This pseudo-light can be best obtained from the underpainting by simply wiping off the wet overpaint with a piece of cheesecloth (we are already familiar with this manipulation). Or the light effects can be lightly brushed into the wet glaze.

Painting clothing

And now we return to the nature of our underpainting for the accessories. We find that under the blue color of the turban (mixed from umber, ultramarine, and white), a pink was used (Venetian red and white); under the yellow of the dress, a darker brownish hue of the yellow (ochre, umber, a trace of Venetian red, and white) was chosen. Like the shadows of the flesh, the shadow area of the dress was glazed with umber, and the lights were painted opaquely with ochre and white.

The light blue of the turban is entirely opaque, but the shadow part is painted so thinly that the pink of the underpainting registers ever so slightly. You can also see that the white of the collar was underpainted in a dark, bluish gray—the actual color of white as it appears in shade. Here, the pure white was brushed in only as a finishing touch, leaving the gray of the underpainting as the final color.

The background was painted as dark as it appears in the Vermeer picture (umber, ultramarine, and a trace of white).

Thus only four colors were used to paint this picture. If you ask me now whether this was the way the original 17th century painting was done, I shall answer yes.

Corrections and retouching

If the work appears satisfactory after the first color treatment, you are a lucky portraitist. More likely, however, corrections of one kind or another will be needed. How shall you go about it? If you have used the suggested colors under normal circumstances, the painting should be dry the following day and could be retouched or overpainted as desired. As for retouching, a small round sable brush—carefully and judiciously used on spots previously moistened by the medium—can produce radical changes in linear definitions.

Repainting surfaces *already* painted is another matter. To do this properly, you must pretend that you are working on a surface which is still wet. Take the shadow side for example. Should you wish to make it lighter, first you must place an identical color on the existing dry color, after moistening the surface with the medium. Then, gradually, you may lighten the fresh color. To make light areas still lighter, use the same procedure.

When you attempt to make the shadows darker, this procedure is not required; for here the application of a darker glaze on top of the original color will produce the desired effect. No particular preparation is needed except that the surface should be oiled.

A finished dry portrait may require softening of the contours—the interior outlines such as those around the eyelids and the lips, or the contour of the head against the background. For the eyelids, a round sable brush will make them softer if you use a color lighter than the one used for the original outline. The *outer* contour, of the head, however, will have to be treated in a different manner. If you are to properly blend the paint of the hair or the cheek (that forms the outer contour) into the background, the background must be wet. Place a narrow strip of fresh paint on both

the surfaces to be blended—where they meet —and this will allow you to make the contours as fuzzy as you wish.

Background colors

Even a plain background that is nothing but a colored surface may be a problem. Many artists attempt to finish the background *before* they paint the head because that was how they were taught in art schools. Actually, the background is the *last* element to be considered in portraiture because its colors and its light and shade arrangement must be adjusted to the appearance of the central figure on stage— your model. The background must *enhance* all that is attractive in the model.

Here, we shall discuss plain backdrops, as we may call them, whose light and shade were mentioned in Chapter 11. Our first question is: what color should we choose? Previously, I have expressed my preference for relatively neutral colors. But there are a number of categories of neutral coloring.

We must decide first whether to choose a cool or warm color scheme. If we use a cool background of bluish or greenish domination, we must be aware that it will make the flesh tint appear warmer by contrast. The background color can materially influence the tonality of the flesh color.

What, then, is the range of the blue and green tonalities that we can consider for our backgrounds? The components of a blue-gray are Prussian blue, umber, and white. Green-grays can be mixed from Prussian blue, ochre, umber, and white. These could be considered the principal mixtures.

There are also subsidiary combinations. Gray can be mixed from viridian green, umber, and white. Green-gray can be mixed from viridian green, ochre, umber, and white; or black, ochre, and white.

On rare occasions, the following color mixtures could be considered: viridian green, Venetian red, and white; Prussian blue, Venetian red, and white; Prussian blue, Venetian red, ochre, and white.

On small paintings, where the head occupies most of the surface—that is, where the background is inconspicuous—a strong background color, such as pure cadmium red or a strong blue, can be used to advantage. On large surfaces, this does not work because the strong color overwhelms the figure, unless the figure is also treated in high-keyed colors.

All the colors I have discussed—with the exception of cadmium red—are of cool tonality. You may ask, how about the warm tonalities? These would be arrived at from mixtures of burnt umber, burnt siena, Venetian or Indian red, and related colors. I can see backgrounds of such colors only on an official portrait—a bank president, a chairman of the board, or perhaps the Postmaster General.

One more problem: does the color of the sitter (complexion, hair, etc.) influence the color of the background? On rare occasions, it would. Red hair, for example, would be "glorified" by a blue-green background. And most assuredly, the color of a gown will dictate the choice of a particular color scheme in a picture —provided that the gown dominates the scheme of a painting.

Glazing and scumbling backgrounds

All the mixtures I have discussed represent opaque applications. You may ask, how about glazes? Can these be used in painting backgrounds? When used on large surfaces, glazes do not work well. An effective glaze should be luminous and this luminosity makes the glaze too strong for our purpose. But, when confined to small areas, transparent or semi-transparent glazes can be quite effective.

My reluctance to discuss glazes for backgrounds gives way to enthusiasm when I mention scumbling, for this operation is made to order for the occasion. Where else do we have a surface that can be worked over with the knife from top to bottom and across with complete abandon?

Now that I have mentioned knives (the painting knife for small areas and the blender for large surfaces), I must stress that these are

the finest instruments for painting backgrounds. In fact, in my own work, I hardly ever use a brush for this purpose.

Either the knife or brush (should you be partial to the latter) will obviously be moved on the surface in some fashion. Thus, the mark of the knife or the brush will register on the canvas, creating definite textures, unless you belong to the school that favors only smooth surfaces like those produced by a spray gun. This does not mean, however, that perfectly smooth backgrounds are to be ruled out entirely—far from it!

In regard to these background marks, experience teaches us that certain rules must be observed. These are illustrated in Fig. 54.

When I mention the forbidding term, *rules*, I do it after much soul searching, for all rules are just the strictures which a genius would break successfully. However, it is not the intention of this book to spawn geniuses; all we aim at is to produce good paintings of people as we know them in everyday life.

Consequently, we shall have to adhere to certain rules. Here are a few. Do not let your brush stroke slide up and down vertically on your background. Do not allow your brush to fly in every direction. High impasti in the background and a smooth treatment of the flesh will create an unpleasant disparity of textural effects; in other words, impasti in the background should not exceed those used elsewhere in the picture. In fact, it is always safer to keep the background "becalmed," even if the figure shows an agitated treatment.

I have discussed all kinds of backgrounds but one: the uniformly dark, nearly black backdrop seen on certain old masters. I did use it once, when trying to follow Vermeer's ideas (Color Plate 12), but in contemporary portraiture, I would rule it out.

Backgrounds and accessories

By accessories, we mean the costume and other items that may enrich the composition by transforming a plain background into an interior or even a landscape. As I have said, it is

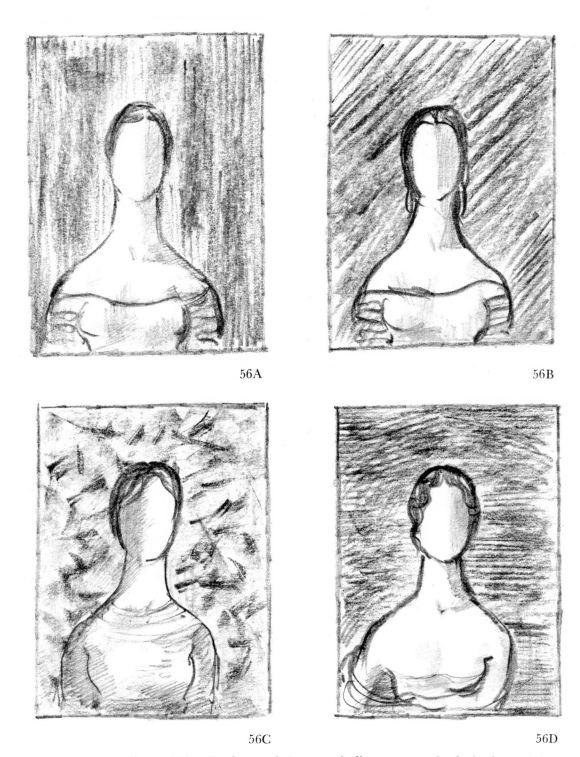

56A   56B

56C   56D

Figure 56A. *Strokes carried out vertically seem to make the background drip downward. 56B. Diagonal strokes seem to be pushing the model out of her rightful place. 56C. Here the marks of the brush or knife take on a definitely belligerent attitude against the model. 56D. The background demarcations spell tranquility, order, and harmony. The vertical position of the figure is counterbalanced by the predominantly—but not obtrusively —horizontal movement of the background.*

pointless to imitate the classic conceptions of the Renaissance or the Baroque, where landscape or interior backgrounds were standard. In short, do not drag false grandeur and histrionics into the scene; better limit yourself to plain backgrounds.

The fundamentals of costume were mentioned in Chapter 11; we shall now discuss the treatment of costume in color. In this area, calligraphic effects can be produced by using the scriptliner—the instrument that we have not, as yet, had the opportunity to use. This brush—unlike any other brush—can give us sustained draftsman-like effects.

Much as I would be tempted to suggest ways to "dress up the model," these would be of no real value to the student. Let me repeat the (by now) familiar advice: avoid modish extravagance. Whether you paint male or female attire, reduce it to its simplest, most basic forms.

Here are a few rules regarding the interrelation of costume and the human form.

(1) Do not put so much emphasis on the costume that it becomes more important, or more conspicuous than the wearer.

(2) Avoid high-pitched colors.

(3) Treat garments casually and sketchily; do not rely on details and precision in painting the folds. Exactness in execution will make the work appear tedious, pedantic, or dull.

(4) Avoid that perfect finish which, almost always, will stultify the beholder's imagination. In the treatment of nonessential details, suggestions are more eloquent than precise elaborations.

After you have considered these maxims, let us proceed with the technicalities. Should the costume—or shall we call it dress—be painted in impasto or glazes? Strong impasti will, most certainly, put a smoothly painted face at a disadvantage; glazes will do better in this respect. As a matter of fact, although glazes serve us poorly when they are used in backgrounds, they are perfectly at home used on fabrics draped around the model.

Thus, for the treatment of accessories, consider glazes and linear definitions. Both these techniques are highly compatible, and when used skillfully and with discrimination, they may imbue your work with animation and spirit.

Here are some suggestions for glazing.

(1) Pale yellow underpainting; viridian or burnt siena (and black) glaze.

(2) Strong yellow underpainting; umber and ultramarine glaze.

(3) Red underpainting; viridian or dark green glaze.

(4) Viridian underpainting; cadmium red glaze.

(5) Light gray underpainting; alizarin crimson (and black) glaze.

(6) Light pink underpainting; viridian (and black) glaze.

These are a few suggestions which, depending on the quantity or dominance of one color or another, will yield endless coloristic variations.

What about using scumbling for painting draperies? If done with a slight impasto into the wet glaze, they are very effective. But when you use the painting knife and stronger impasti, scumbles are only practical on small surfaces such as scarves, veils, and the like. However, when it is used for curvilinear definitions on larger surfaces, the painting knife becomes a recalcitrant tool—not recommended.

Chapter 15

Painting
alla prima

Alla prima is an ancient technique, dating back to the 15th century, if we consider its most famous early champion, Hieronymus Bosch. However, there can be little doubt that alla prima painting was known long before then. For all practical purposes, we shall look to Rubens (16th-17th centuries) as its foremost proponent because our own procedure will be identical with that seen in his work.

What is alla prima painting?

This technique relies on a one-phase operation —on *finishing work while painting wet-in-wet,* without prior underpainting. Since your paint dries within a day, this means that your work must be finished in a matter of hours. Once the paint dries, overpaints in this technique are not feasible, as this would destroy the characteristic appearance of the painting; minor retouchings can be done, however, as I shall explain later.

What, then, are the characteristics of an alla prima painting? They are spontaneity, freshness, sketchiness; its predominant transparency makes it kindred (in a fashion) to watercolor. Just as in watercolor—where the white of the paper shows here and there and appears, somewhat, through the thin layer of colors—in alla prima painting, the imprimatura shows up through the overpaint, besides being visible on small spots not covered up by paint.

What are the limitations of the technique? It is really best for sizes not larger than about 16″ x 20″, preferably smaller. Large paintings appear tenuous when they are executed thinly on an imprimatura. Moreover, speed in execution presupposes assured draftsmanship; for this reason, painting a portrait alla prima is not a method to be attempted by the beginner.

A thing to remember: when you paint alla prima, your brushes, knives, oil cup, and the surface of the panel and palette must be absolutely free from dust. Otherwise, these impurities will make themselves unpleasantly felt on the finished painting because of the thinness and transparency of the glaze. As you will see, glazes predominate when you paint in this technique.

Panels for alla prima painting

Panels are the ideal surface for alla prima technique. However, when you work on a panel, the use of the painting knife is limited and altogether difficult because there is no give and take between the elastic blade and the rigid surface. Why, then, do we have to rely on a rigid surface, that is, on a panel support?

At one time, when traditional gesso (white pigment dispersed in glue size) was the only ground available, a rigid support was imperative because the inelastic gesso would easily crack on a flexible canvas. This limitation does

113

not exist any longer, as our new acrylic gesso can be safely applied to a canvas. However, there remains one important advantage in using a panel—its smooth surface. Why is the smooth surface of the panel so desirable? Simply because every brushstroke registers on it incisively and immediately; there are no declivities and hillocks (like the interstices of the canvas) to impede the movement of the brush. Because of this regularity, the round sable brush—preferable for painting alla prima —becomes just as important as the bristle brush.

Because of the paint's thinness in alla prima technique, increased viscosity (allowing paint to acquire a heavier body) is essential. Therefore, we shall use the Copal Painting Medium Heavy to dilute the paint, and we shall condition every color—as it comes from the tube —with a little Copal Concentrate, just as we do when we paint on canvas.

Preparing the panel

Untempered Masonite, ⅛″ thick, is our best choice. Only the smooth side of the panel should be used; it can be gessoed without any preliminaries. As I have mentioned, our present day acrylic material, known in the trade as acrylic gesso, is best for our purpose. This compound is too thick to be used straight from the can (as suggested on the label) because when this thick substance is brushed on it will leave brush marks which would adversely affect the texture of subsequent painting. The gesso must be thinned to the consistency of milk, and three separate applications will be required to produce an opaque film. As the material dries rapidly, these layers can be painted on in short intervals.

To prevent the panel from warping, which sometimes occurs, I would advise that you prime it on both sides simultaneously. The gesso priming should be applied with an ordinary small housepainter's brush; no sandpapering will be required.

Now you may ask why you cannot buy prepared panels, obtainable in every art store?

Even assuming that such panels carry the proper gesso priming (which is not always the case), their surface appears mechanically even because the gesso material is sprayed on. On such panels, thinly executed paintings take on an excessively slick look.

Imprimatura

A panel prepared with acrylic gesso is non-absorbent to a certain degree, but not sufficiently so to be painted over with oil colors. Moreover, its white surface would not be too attractive; or rather, it would not lend its own color to the subsequent painting. Therefore, after priming, the panel should first receive a thin film of transparent color, which we call *imprimatura*. The imprimatura is, in fact, a glaze. But whereas the glaze is thinned with the medium, an imprimatura employs *varnish* as a thinner. Only copal varnish described in Chapter 9 is suitable for this purpose.

Why is the copal imprimatura superior to any other treatment of the gesso ground? Why could we not, for instance, use damar varnish instead? Outwardly, damar will produce the same effect, but damar never solidifies to an impervious film—no matter how long it is allowed to dry. If we paint on a damar imprimatura with our Copal Painting Medium, the damar varnish, no matter how old, will be dissolved by the turpentine which the medium contains. The copal varnish imprimatura, on the other hand, can be safely overpainted after two days.

Could we use turpentine or linseed oil for diluting our imprimatura colors? Turpentine possesses no binding power, and no capacity to isolate the gesso—that is, to reduce its absorbency. Linseed oil is too "fat"; therefore, it is totally unsuitable for our purpose at this early stage, when the painting should be "lean" (containing a minimum of oil) rather than "fat" (rich in oil), a quality reserved for the final paint layers. (This "fat over lean" principle is essential for permanency.)

How would acrylic colors work when used for an imprimatura application? Very well, indeed, except that they would bring about a reduction in the ground's luminosity; as we know, the luminous quality of the imprimatura is of paramount importance in the alla prima technique.

In our pro and con discussion, we did not consider an oil priming for gesso panels. Such a priming (the same as used for canvases) is acceptable, but it has neither the glowing, light-reflective power of the gesso, nor is it easy to produce a smooth surface by brushing oil paint onto a panel. And if we dilute the oil paint, the loss of its opacity would immediately rule it out as a foundation.

And now for the choice of a color for the imprimatura. Which one will be most suitable? Unhesitatingly, I would say *burnt siena*. This hue will provide the panel with a rich, glowing, reddish brown film of great transparency. A duller but also useful color will be obtained from *burnt umber*. Burnt siena and burnt umber are the principal imprimatura colors when you paint a portrait. However, the experienced painter, bent on experimentation within reasonable limits, may consider *viridian green*, which could be used *alone* or placed *under* or *over* burnt siena or burnt umber. This paint overlay should be done on a dry surface. You can also use a mixture of these colors.

Alla prima technique

The imprimatura dries sufficiently in two days or more. It can be made to dry much faster when you use cobalt dryer. Then you can start your drawing using vine charcoal; its marks are later made indelible with fixative.

The next step is to *oil the panel with your medium*. This measure is absolutely essential because, without it, you would experience difficulties in painting. After the oiling, the originally flat surface—of whatever color—will become lustrous. Instead of oiling, you may use a glaze which, in effect, is oiling with color. Thus, the burnt siena imprimatura can be glazed with the same color, or with umber. Here the painter may follow his impulse; as-

suming that he is conversant with the alla prima method, his impulse will not lead him astray.

As usual, start painting the shadows. On a burnt siena imprimatura, these may seem to take on a bilious color at the beginning, even though you may have enough red in your mixture. But do not become alarmed. As soon as the imprimatura begins to disappear under your overpaint, the color will start looking up. The reason is that the glowing color of burnt siena throws even a warm flesh color out of kilter; but as soon as you paint the background in blue or green, the healthy complexion of your model will automatically reappear.

In Color Plate 13A, the first phase of the painting (on a burnt umber imprimatura) is represented. In Color Plate 13B, the lights have been added, but both the light and shade still appear understated. In Color Plate 13C, blending has been done with a bristle brush (the shadows as well as the lights), and the drawing has been strengthened; the background was painted with cadmium red. For the flesh colors, our usual combination was used.

Can the blending of colors be carried out on a panel with the *knife*? The answer is—*no*. When the paint is moved by the knife, the wet color has no place to go but to slither about on the surface; there are no interstices to take it up. But the knife can be used judiciously and skillfully here and there. On the demonstration panel, we see its marks on the background.

Color Plate 14 shows the characteristic appearance of an alla prima work, with all its salient features. The brownish color of the imprimatura prevails throughout the entire panel, showing up sporadically in smaller and larger spots, thus tying up the tonality of the whole. In addition, the picture appears sketchy; glazes prevail over opaque passages; and linear definitions are stressed. It is interesting, perhaps, to mention that it required forty minutes to complete this work, from the beginning to the final touches. One of the great virtues of the classic alla prima technique—for the busy portrait painters of the past—is speed.

Painting alla prima on canvas

After reading my discussion of alla prima painting, you may assume that a canvas cannot be used for this purpose. Well, it can if certain requirements are met, although such a painting may be termed alla prima in name only. It will be a one phase operation, but its appearance and its technique will differ from our orthodox procedures which rely on precepts established by the Rubens school.

To begin with, the canvas will have to be very smooth, its texture nearly silken. The priming will be opaque, and—to name the one easiest to handle—prepared from umber and white. (As you may remember, I mentioned that Gainsborough preferred such a priming; Goya more often chose a red ground.) The painting on such primings is carried out in one operation; white is used in mixtures to a much larger extent than in work done on the panel because the ground provides no luminosity from within. As usual, on a canvas, the painting knife can be used without restraint.

To fully understand the character of alla prima work on canvas, it is best to study paintings of the masters done in this manner. There is one cardinal difference between painting alla prima on canvas and on a panel. As I mentioned, if we overpaint a work on a panel, it will at once lose its intrinsic characteristics of immediacy and sketchiness. This is not so when you paint on a canvas, which *can* be overpainted. A canvas can be painted alla prima but not look it; it is not the appearance of the work which stamps it categorically as an alla prima work, but the *method*. In fact, the alla prima character of the canvas will not be recognized by anyone but the informed, practicing painter. (See Plates 25 and 31.)

Chapter 16

Gallery of great portraits

Now we shall review portraits conceived through the periods when portraiture became a major branch of painting. This is not to say that portrait painting was unknown in antiquity; but except for work done in stone (preserved in enormous quantities), very few examples of ancient painting remain in existence. Why should reference to the past be important? Because, as I mentioned at the onset of this book, the past is the only source from which we may gather understanding of the pictorial problems that face us. Hence, we shall now seek out precedents—typical portraits against which we may gauge our own conceptions and from which we may gain a sense of direction.

Early Renaissance portraits

To begin at the beginning, Pollaiuolo (Plate 15), Botticelli (Plate 16), Memling (Plate 17), and Holbein (Plate 18) represent the earliest types of Renaissance portraiture, although they are not all in the same style because their countries of origin differ. All these examples are crisp, hard renditions, *linear* rather than *painterly* in character. In fact, artists of later generations used to say that work done in this manner was "tinted with colors, not painted" because these paintings are smooth and lack the texture of brush strokes. That is, the brush was not used freely; a meticulous drawing was,

in a more or less miniaturistic fashion, "colored." Paintings of this nature were not done on canvas, but on wooden panels which lent themselves much better to work relying on precise execution of minutiae.

Of the portraits now under discussion, the most decorative is the one by Botticelli (Plate 16) because of the splendor of the dress and the headgear and the extraordinary calligraphy of the linear patterns. Representations in profile lend themselves particularly well to such treatment, since their flat surface, rather than their three-dimensional form, is stressed.

The portrait by Pollaiuolo (Plate 15) is obviously done in tempera and, in its emphasis on line, typifies early Florentine portraiture. On the other hand, the Memling (Plate 17), a product of the Flemish school, is really late Gothic in spirit and technique. One might think that this panel also carries a tempera foundation because of the outward appearance of the painting. However, this must be ruled out; much earlier work done by Van Eyck, the founder of the Flemish school, proved to have been executed only with oil colors, on the basis of microchemical examination carried out some years ago.

A portrait *par excellence* is the Holbein (Plate 18). One is aware that this is the work of a specialist of the highest order. The other painters previously mentioned—although endowed with genius—were more like "general practitioners," doing paintings of all kinds. But Holbein stuck to portraits only, with a singular capacity for characterization. Conspicuous in all work of that era is the lack of a pronounced chiaroscuro; that is, there are no strong contrasts between light and shade areas. These contrasts were not sought after.

Can we base our work on these conceptions? Not very well, for the element of decor, which was part and parcel of the style, can no longer be exploited.

High Renaissance portraits

When Titian (Plates 19 and 20) was middle aged, he discovered the charm conveyed by brush strokes. This interest contrasted sharply with the earlier school of painting which aimed at perfectly smooth paint surfaces. However, compared to Velazquez (Plates 21 and 22), Titian's bravura in handling the brush was moderate indeed. In the strictest sense, it may not be quite accurate to classify these painters as part of the High Renaissance, since Titian, in his long lifespan, reached well into the age of the Baroque—the period in which Velazquez was born. Yet, in the work of both these painters, the characteristic configurations of the Baroque style are strangely absent.

Quite early in his career, Velazquez adopted an almost impressionistic brush stroke and a disdain for the pedantic treatment of details. From an artistic viewpoint, which are greater, his earlier achievements or his later work? The answer is that both his impressionistic and classical treatments are of the highest artistic order. Looking at these two approaches analytically, we could say that the sketchy treatment completely renders the artist's own, inimitable handwriting, whereas the carefully executed earlier paintings lack this characteristic.

Baroque portraits

Of all the Baroque painters, Rubens (Plates 23 and 24) was the most typical of his period and, as such, he overstated the corporeality of his subjects and overcharged their fleshiness with pulsating life. Frans Hals (Plates 25 and 26) never shunned appearing florid; but this ruddy quality is still more strongly apparent in Rubens. Recall once more the principles of technique exposed in this treatise; they conform to those found in Rubens' work. However, this does not imply that we want to overstate the fleshiness of our models. Far from it; you may use the same technique in painting the deadest rock or wicker basket.

With Frans Hals, the virtuoso stroke of the brush reached its highest potential. The life-size painting in Plate 25 was executed alla prima on a brownish toned ground; it must have been a work of only a few hours. The slashing strokes of the brush race over the canvas with an imperious authority never attained by any other painter before or after him. Observe the treatment of the hands; they are but a web of loose brush strokes. Could we follow Hals' precepts? Hardly; one cannot adopt the personal handwriting of someone else.

In Rubens, the Baroque found its most eloquent protagonist (this, of course, is less apparent in his portrait work than in his figure and landscape compositions). Again, we wonder if Rubens can serve as a model for our own work? The affirmative answer can be found in the chapter on alla prima painting. Furthermore, our method of underpainting and overpainting follows procedures similar to those used by his school. And since Rubens' art, unlike that of Frans Hals, is not rooted in the brush stroke bravura style, Rubens' technique may well be emulated by the contemporary portraitist.

Who could deny Rembrandt's supremacy as an artist (Plates 27 and 28)? His best paintings have (to use a word now under strictest embargo) soul. Could we produce this ingredient by a mere act of will? Certainly not; soulfulness cannot be ordered. Could we employ his colors and his method of illumination? No, we could not do this very well in contemporary portraiture.

Now for the Vermeer (Plate 29) which served as the model for my color demonstration. Why have I chosen this particular painting? It is one of my great favorites; whenever I face it in the Mauritshuis, in the Hague, the painting's charm entrances me. My picture, however, is not an exact copy. First, I could not make myself follow the smooth handling seen in the original. And then there is the mouth, so characteristic of this painting; it is slightly open, with a glimpse of teeth. I cannot see any such conception being used nowadays, simply because it injects a naturalistic note into the picture.

What did I learn from this masterpiece? A very important lesson of simplification. On the nose, observe the contour that faces the source of light: the expected definition of form is just not there; the light eats up the detail. This, in itself, might seem to be only of slight importance; but, for me, it was a revelation.

Referring once again to my demonstration, based on Vermeer, I must reemphasize the fact that the old masters almost always used a grisaille underpainting in executing commissioned portraits. When the exigencies of a commission were not present, or when the artist felt perfectly at ease, work was often done alla prima on a canvas carrying a toned ground.

Goya

From Vermeer, we move ahead in time almost a hundred years to the master whose artistic potential equals that of the great geniuses of the past.

Now, Goya's *Don Manuel Osorio* (Plate 30) is a work of great charm; coloristically, it is Goya at his best. But it was painted when he was not yet forty, when his technique was not fully developed. Strangely, if not for the typical "old master" background, the frontal lighting (we may call it *plein air*) and the consequent absence of shadows make us think of Renoir at his best. Also interesting, in this picture, is the use of an old device: the shadow at the bottom of the picture moves the child's figure into the background, thus containing it within the recessional plane.

The next picture (Plate 31) is the best lesson in alla prima painting you can ever receive. It is done on a canvas carrying a toned ground of orange color, a middle tone which was fully utilized in the coloristic rendering of the flesh. The painting of the child's face is like a drawing on colored paper where the highlights of the face are marked with white chalk—the toned ground remained untouched in the shadow part. That is how the face of the child was painted, probably in ten minutes flat.

The face of *Maria Luisa*, however, required more elaborate treatment. Here the orange color of the toned ground was used for transitional tones, mediating between the highlights and the shadows. Observe the painting of the dress: it is scumbled with loose brush strokes into a glaze of wet umber.

As you may have noticed, I did not place Goya specifically in the 18th or 19th century, although his life span straddled both. Since he did not follow fashionable precepts, his period could have been Baroque, Rococo, Neo-Classic, or Romantic—but he chose to be himself.

19th century portraits

Between Goya and our next painter, Manet, lies roughly half a century. Manet's realistic portraiture may be termed "academic" inasmuch as he adhered to traditional precepts. But his technique had neither the authority of Velazquez, whose early manner he tried to adopt, nor the spiritedness of Goya, who also was a source of influence. The portrait in Plate 36 is painted in heavy impasti throughout (without glazing, which he never used) with a broad, energetic brush. Manet shunned commitments to petty details and irrelevancies of all sorts. This simplification accounts for the chief merit of his art. In *Woman with a Parrot*, the frontal light conformed to the mode of his day.

Degas and Renoir were almost the same age and died only two years apart. Degas (Plates 34 and 35) as not only a great portraitist, but a master of pictorial composition, surpassing every one of his contemporaries. By mastery of composition, I do not merely mean the attainment of harmony and balance—a virtue achieved easily, even by the inexperienced; I mean the creation of an original system of composition, which is a very rare feat indeed.

The merit of Degas' portraits lies in their simplicity, economy of means, and reticence—in other words, in their good taste. His technique was exceedingly uncomplicated, and similar to the one advocated in this book, but with one exception. The underpaintings, wherever they occurred, were much more monochromatic; Degas preferred to work alla prima on a light brown toned canvas. Consequently, there is an absence of brilliant glazes, for these presuppose a relatively strong underlying color. When he tired of monotones, Degas resorted to colorful pastels—perhaps to elevate his spirit. Indeed, he was a dour fellow, contemptuous of his public and somewhat of a misanthrope.

Did Renoir (Plates 37 and 38) have genius also? You would not think so if you saw only the work he did after the age of forty. And if you faced only the stuff which he produced somewhat after 1900, you would doubt that he had even a modicum of talent. Yet, in his early work, reproduced here (and in a number of later productions), the quality of his paintings is of the highest order. He was the only Impressionist (if we classify him thus) who used glazes; in his early training as a porcelain painter, he became familiar with this technique. Yet Renoir cannot serve as our example precisely because of his impressionistic touch. As I said before, never try to imitate anyone's handwriting.

Our last example, Plate 39, has always worried me. Sargent was, without doubt, the greatest portraitist of our age, and the portrait of *Mme. X* belongs with the very best (although the picture was rejected as being too provocative by the husband of the lady). To return to my initial puzzlement, why is this portrait not as great as a great Velazquez? Perhaps the table on which the lady rests her arm so theatrically gives us the clue to the dilemma. In what other age could an object so lacking in taste have been designed? It was built in an age without a valid style. Thus it appears that *Mme. X*, which has the painterly virtues of a Velazquez, lacks the sound stylistic ideology prevalent during the time of the great Spanish portraitist. But is this the whole answer? I leave the puzzle to you.

Plate 15. *Antonio Pollaiuolo (1429-1498)*, Portrait of a Lady. *A tempera painting very thinly executed on a white gesso panel without underpainting. Tonal transitions are achieved by delicate cross-hatching produced by a pointed sable brush. In accordance with the prevailing tradition, a heavy, viscous oil paint was used for the background.*

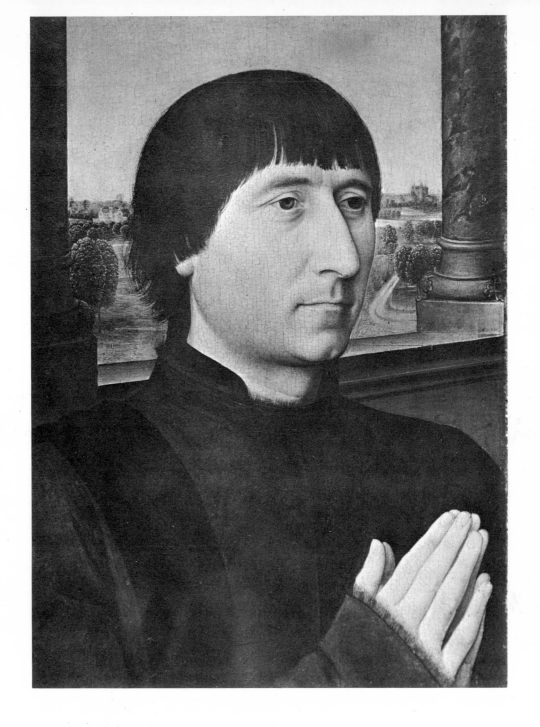

Plate 17. *Hans Memling (1430-1494)*, Guillaume Moreel. *Museum of Ancient Art, Brussels. The system of the early Flemish masters did not differ in principle from that of the Italians, but the style of the northern artists was characteristically Gothic. All objects and details are isolated by an outline, which forms self-contained units; the entire composition is an assembly of independent parts.*

Plate 16. *Sandro Botticelli (1444-1510)*, Simonetta Vespucci. *Dahlem Museum, Berlin. This is an oil painting on a gesso panel—still in the tradition of the earlier tempera technique—which aimed at linear treatment without emphasis on chiaroscuro.*

Detail of Jane Seymour.

Plate 18. *Hans Holbein (1460-1524),* Jane Seymour. *Like the foregoing examples, this relies on a linear conception, avoiding blended contours and stressing minute details with great precision.*

Plate 19.   *Titian (1477-1576),* Man in a Red Cap. *Frick Collection, New York. Note the free, flowing brushwork and delicate textures. This is classic portraiture at its best, with all its attributes of serenity and nobility.*

Detail of Man in Red Cap.

126

128

Plate 21.   *Diego De Silva Velazquez (1599-1660),* Don Gaspar de Guzman *(detail). Metropolitan Museum of Art, New York. Here is a close-up of the Spanish master's brushwork. Compare the soft strokes that make up the texture of the skin and hair with the raggedly painted collar.*

Plate 20.   *Titian (1477-1576),* Karl V *(detail). Alte Pinakothek, Munich. Freeing himself from the archaic influences of the linear painters who preceded him, Titian sought painterly effects and pictorial unity based on tonal values rather than on strident, precisely formulated areas of color defined by sharp edges. His work is rich in soft transitions, and detail is suppressed.*

129

Plate 22. *Diego De Silva Velazquez (1599-1660)*, The Infanta Margarita.
*Art History Museum, Vienna. Observe the impressionistic treatment of
the Infanta's costume and compare it with that of the Holbein painting.
Also note the manner in which the hair is treated; how different it is
from that of Pollaiuolo and Botticelli! All of Velazquez's paintings
were done on canvas.*

Detail of The Infanta Margarita.

130

Plate 24 (Above).   *Peter Paul Rubens (1577-1640),* The Abbott. *State Museum of Art, Copenhagen. With the exception of the head, the hands, and the bishop's hat, this is also painted alla prima on an imprimatura covered gesso panel.*

Plate 23 (Left).   *Peter Paul Rubens (1577-1640),* Portrait of an Old Man. *Metropolitan Museum of Art, New York. This is an alla prima painting on a gesso panel with a burnt siena imprimatura. The shadows are glowing, warm glazes, while the lights are opaque and semi-opaque impasti.*

Plate 25. *Frans Hals (1580-1666),* Malle Babbe. *Metropolitan Museum of Art, New York. An alla prima work on a canvas carrying a thin, dark, brownish tone which allows the white priming to assert itself. The entire picture is built up from a veritable cascade of loose brush strokes.*

Detail of Malle Babbe.

Plate 26. *Frans Hals (1580-1666),* Portrait of a Man *(detail). Metropolitan Museum of Art, New York. This probably took just two sittings: the first a kind of understatement, and the final effects slashed in with a determination that only Frans Hals could assume. Study the crisp accents of light and dark around the eyes, nose, and mouth.*

136

Plate 27.   *Rembrandt van Rijn (1606-1669),* Lucretia *(detail). Minneapolis Institute of Arts. This close-up gives an excellent view of this master's rich paint texture. Compare the pattern of light and shade on the head with the mnemonic patterns in Chapter 7.*

Detail of **Flora.**

138

Plate 28. *Rembrandt van Rijn (1606-1669),* Flora. *Metropolitan Museum of Art, New York. No, he did not have Frans Hals' capacity for hitting "bullseyes" whenever he wielded his brush, but his imagination traveled beyond the limits of the image; he most assuredly was a greater artist than Frans Hals. Both* Flora *and* Lucretia *are the results of many overpaintings, whence comes their intrinsic energy, the massive internal energy that flows from the spirit—a quality that cannot be achieved by mere virtuosity.*

140

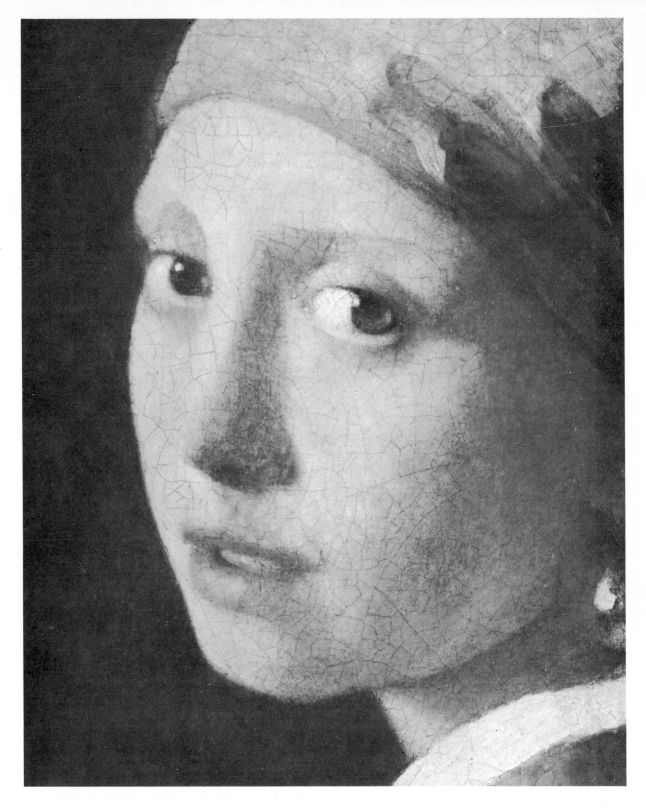

Detail of Head of a Girl with Blue Turban.

Plate 29. *Jan Vermeer (1632-1675),* Head of a Girl with Blue Turban.
*Mauritshuis, The Hague. One of the most charming portraits in all
art history—not just because of the appeal of the model, but because of
the picture's lighting, color, and utter simplicity of means.*

EL S.^R D.^N MANVEL OSORIO MANRRIQVE ⅁ ZVÑIGA S.^N D GINES NACIO EN A^S. A J J D 1784

Plate 30. *Francisco de Goya (1746-1828),* Don Manuel Osorio.
*Metropolitan Museum of Art, New York. This is the artist's youthful
work, and it almost presages Renoir. The light enters the scene from the
front, thus failing to create chiaroscuro. Hence, the painter could
concentrate on color: the pearly complexion of the child, his dazzling
sash, and the brilliant vermilion of his dress.*

142

Plate 31. *Francisco de Goya (1746-1828),* The Infanta Maria Luisa.
Metropolitan Museum of Art, New York. Unlike Don Manuel Osorio, *the
portrait of* Maria Luisa *is an alla prima work executed on a red
ground, in perhaps three hours. Most assuredly, it is not the speed that
impresses us, but the brilliant technical performance and keen
resourcefulness which I described earlier in the text.*

Plate 32. *Thomas Gainsborough (1728-1788),* Richard Paul Jodrell *(detail). Frick Collection, New York. Here is Rococo elegance at its most polished and refined. If the artist worked on this head for more than one sitting, he did hardly anything but retouch the alla prima conception at the second sitting. It is not an exaggeration to say that the original condition of the canvas contributes largely to the final appearance. The fabric is of silken fineness and carries a light umber color. This color remains scarcely touched in the shadow part of the man's face and his powdered wig.*

144

Plate 33. *Thomas Gainsborough (1728-1788), Mrs. Elliott (detail). Frick Collection, New York. The toned ground carries no underpainting. Her face, however, is not quite alla prima; the enameled complexion had to be worked over twice, at least.*

Plate 35 (Above). *Edgar Degas (1834-1917)*, Portrait of the Artist.
Metropolitan Museum of Art, New York. In both paintings reproduced
here, the artist did not deviate from classic precepts. In the self-portrait, the
chief effect is derived from the exploitation of the chiaroscuro and its
strong values of dark and light. These values are simplified to a point
where details become almost completely subdued by either light or shadow.
The simplification is apparent in every area of the painting.

Plate 34 (Left). *Edgar Degas (1834-1917)*, Portrait of a Lady in Gray.
Metropolitan Museum of Art, New York. In this portrait, we must admire
how cunningly the artist went about making an attractive picture out
of the ungainly appearance of the model. Note the blurred mellowness
of the contours.

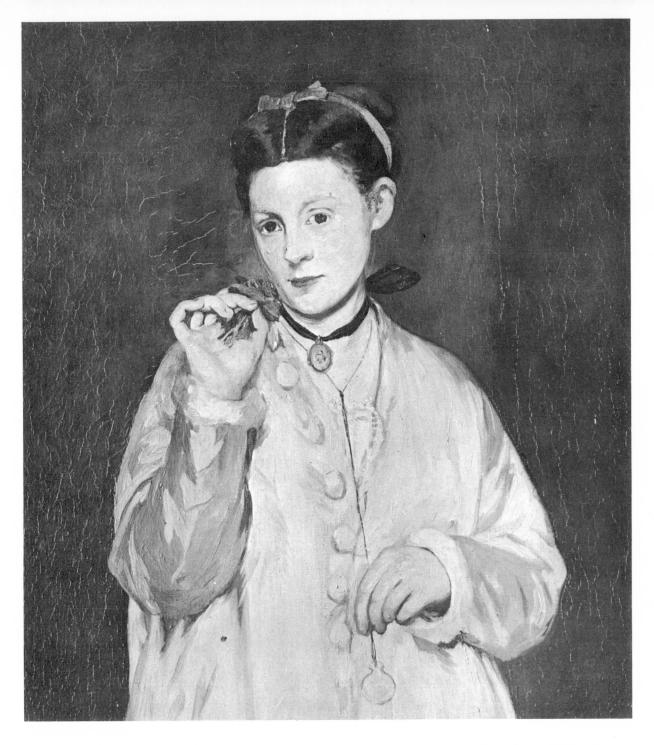

Detail of Woman With a Parrot.

Plate 36. *Edouard Manet (1832-1883),* Woman With a Parrot. *Metropolitan Museum of Art, New York. Manet's* Woman With a Parrot *is a straightforward, skillful impasto painting, closely following the concept of the early Velazquez, except for the consciously used frontal lighting. The artist's vigor is evident in his broad treatment, employing a large, paint-loaded brush.*

Plate 37. *Pierre Auguste Renoir (1841-1919)*, Mme. Charpentier and Her
Children. *I have, on several occasions, stressed the danger of painting
modish attires and fashionable interiors. In this family portrait, everything
is fashionable according to the dictates of the day (the late 1870s), when
taste in these matters had reached point zero. Yet, all is charm in this
work—by virtue of the supremely beautiful handling of the paint.*

Detail of Mme. Charpentier and Her Children.

152

Detail of The Loge.

Plate 38. *Pierre Auguste Renoir (1841-1919),* The Loge. *Courtauld
Institute, London. The same can be said of* The Loge, *also done when the
artist was at the height of his faculties. The sensuous, mellow texture
of the paint is especially worth studying.*

Detail of Madame X.

Plate 39. *John Singer Sargent (1856-1925),* Madame X. *Metropolitan
Museum of Art, New York. Here is early 20th century conservative
portraiture at its best. Conventional painting? Yes, but this one
employs the best convention.*

Index

Edited by Wilma Holden

Designed by James Craig

Composed in eleven point Baskerville by Atlantic Linotype Co., Inc.

Printed and Bound in Japan by Toppan Printing Co., Ltd.